Praise for *The Power of Integrated Learning*

"Anyone who wants to see the best that American higher education can offer will find it on display in this fine book. By telling stories from the diverse institutions in the New American Colleges and Universities consortium, William Sullivan shows high ideals at work every day."—*Edward L. Ayers, President Emeritus, University of Richmond*

"I would highly recommend this book to anyone interested in fostering and building a more integrated and coherent college experience."—*Ken Bain, Author of* What the Best College Teachers Do *and* What the Best College Students Do

"With his usual grace and clarity, William Sullivan has made a compelling case for integrated learning. His study of 25 higher education institutions that comprise the organization of New American Colleges and Universities illustrates the value of not only these institutions but also an engaged liberal arts for students and society in general. This is a most useful book for prospective students, parents, teachers, and counselors, as well as anyone interested in learning about the potential of American higher education to contribute to a better world."—*Ira Harkavy, Associate Vice President, Founding Director, Barbara and Edward Netter Center for Community Partnerships, University of Pennsylvania*

"This volume tells the story of the first group of colleges in the United States to recognize that it is possible for a college to provide high quality education in both the liberal arts and the professions and that this admixture also can increase the exercise of civic responsibility by students and recent graduates. Since those early days, the New American Colleges and Universities (NAC&U) model has been adopted by hundreds of other colleges, while the core NAC&U group continues to prosper. William Sullivan tells an inspiring story that counters the false claims of declining quality in American higher education."—*Richard Ekman, President, Council of Independent Colleges*

"AAC&U has declared integrative learning the '21st century liberal art.' Working intensively with faculty, students, and leaders from the New American Colleges and Universities, William Sullivan brings this far-reaching idea brilliantly to life. Through dozens of curricular, pedagogical, and student vignettes, he shows liberal education at its finest. Readers will find in these pages compelling evidence that creating connections across disciplines, between the liberal arts and professional studies, and between the college and the wider community is the most powerful way to help students chart a course for life and develop their capacities to make a positive difference in the wider world."—*Carol Geary Schneider, President, Association of American Colleges & Universities*

THE POWER OF INTEGRATED LEARNING

THE POWER OF INTEGRATED LEARNING

Higher Education for Success in Life, Work, and Society

William M. Sullivan

1996–2016 20TH ANNIVERSARY

Stylus
PUBLISHING, LLC.

STERLING, VIRGINIA

Sty/us

Published by Stylus Publishing, LLC.
22883 Quicksilver Drive
Sterling, Virginia 20166-2102

Library of Congress Cataloging-in-Publication Data
Names: Sullivan, William M.
Title: The power of integrated learning : higher education for
success in life, work, and society / William M. Sullivan.
Description: Sterling, Virginia : Stylus Publishing, 2016. |
Includes bibliographical references and index.
Identifiers: LCCN 2015044723 (print) |
LCCN 2015045260 (ebook) |
   ISBN 9781620364079 (cloth : alk. paper) |
   ISBN 9781620364086 (pbk. : alk. paper) |
   ISBN 9781620364093 (library networkable e-edition) |
   ISBN 9781620364109 (consumer e-edition)
Subjects: LCSH: New American Colleges and Universities
Consortium. | University cooperation--United States. | Consortia.
Classification: LCC LB2331.5 .S85 2016 (print) |
LCC LB2331.5 (ebook) | DDC 378/.01--dc23
LC record available at http://lccn.loc.gov/2015044723

13-digit ISBN: 978-1-62036-407-9 (cloth)
13-digit ISBN: 978-1-62036-408-6 (paperback)
13-digit ISBN: 978-1-62036-409-3 (library networkable e-edition)
13-digit ISBN: 978-1-62036-410-9 (consumer e-edition)

Printed in the United States of America

All first editions printed on acid-free paper
that meets the American National Standards Institute
Z39-48 Standard.

Bulk Purchases

Quantity discounts are available for use in workshops and for
staff development.
Call 1-800-232-0223

First Edition, 2016

10   9   8   7   6   5   4   3   2   1

To the students, faculty, and staff who contributed to this study, with appreciation for their achievements and gratitude for their goodwill.

CONTENTS

INTRODUCTION

The 25 member institutions of the New American Colleges and Universities (NAC&U) consortium profess dedication to a common aim: to provide their students with an education that integrates the liberal arts, professional studies, and civic responsibility. This is a powerful educational agenda with roots in the long tradition of American undergraduate education. It was updated two decades ago by a group of educational leaders headed by Ernest Boyer, president of the Carnegie Foundation for the Advancement of Teaching, when they launched the NAC&U. Over the intervening two decades the importance of this agenda has increased, while research has provided growing evidence for the effectiveness and value of the sort of integrated approach to college learning the NAC&U model embodies.

My purpose in this book is twofold. First, I want to explore how this agenda is lived across the variety of campuses that belong to the NAC&U consortium. Second, I want to interpret the implications' of that experience for rethinking the model of American undergraduate education more broadly. I believe these implications become clearer when the NAC&U experience is examined within the larger context of what is known today about the best ways to promote undergraduate learning and prepare students for productive and fulfilling lives.

If you are looking for a college that seriously tries to integrate the liberal arts, professional studies, and civic responsibility, I invite you to read further. Take a look at the campuses, the faculty, and the students described in this book. Consider the kind of educational experience these institutions aim to provide.

I also invite you to read about how such an integrated model works, how it draws on the best current understanding of how college adds value to students' lives, and how it illustrates more general principles for improving and reshaping American undergraduate education.

Higher education professionals have not always been effective at explaining the aims of higher education and how they are trying to accomplish its goals. This has become evident in the face of pressures to narrow what college can provide to job skills alone. These pressures threaten the distinctive genius of American higher education, a tradition that has sought to devise educational models appropriate to time, place, and student needs. There has never been only one model. But it is vital today to stress American higher education's aim of enabling students to better understand themselves and their world, to prepare themselves for careers in that world, and to live in ways that benefit not only themselves and their families but also the larger society they will join.

This book explores one group of institutions committed to developing a model of undergraduate education to fulfill those purposes. I have undertaken this book in a spirit of inquiry. However, it is not a work of social science, nor is it wholly impartial. I would like the NAC&U ideal of education to succeed, but I also believe that the cause of higher education, and ultimately the interests of the NAC&U institutions themselves, is best served by honest scrutiny. In the following chapters, I present documented examples and cases, drawn from the range of NAC&U campuses. I hope to convey something of what it is like to experience this kind of education. To clarify what is at stake in these experiences, I take a step back to view examples through the lens of contemporary research on learning and student development. In doing this, I also ask which aspects of the NAC&U examples are instances of the core elements of a better model of undergraduate education for our time.

What This Book Explores and Reports

I want to convey at the beginning that fulfilling the mission of the NAC&U is still ongoing and very much under development. It became clear to me from the start that the member institutions are beset with the same challenges that face all universities and colleges of their type and size. Administrators face rising costs that threaten their ability to carry out their mission. They have to worry about their students' ability to pay in difficult economic times, and, because of this, they also confront the challenge of attracting and retaining students from diverse backgrounds and economic situations, all under more intense competitive pressure.

However, as will become evident as we explore dimensions of this kind of education in later chapters, these institutions are also resourceful and innovative. Altogether, they present a positive story about resilience, commitment, and high-quality achievement. It is an inspiring story, and I believe it holds lessons for all of higher education and for the American democracy the consortium was founded to promote and serve. In the following chapters, I emphasize the undergraduate experience and programs but also discuss the graduate programs offered by many NAC&U institutions (see Appendix B). This book concludes by drawing out the elements of this model of undergraduate education, followed by brief profiles of each member institution (see Appendix A). The consortium is made up of the following 25 institutions:

Arcadia University
Belmont University
California Lutheran University
Drury University
Hamline University
Hampton University
John Carroll University
Manhattan College
Nazareth College
North Central College
Ohio Northern University
Pacific Lutheran University
Roger Williams University
Samford University
St. Edward's University
The Sage Colleges
University of Evansville
University of La Verne
University of New Haven
University of Redlands
University of Scranton
Valparaiso University
Wagner College
Westminster College
Widener University

Frames of an NAC&U Education: The Plan of the Book

This book consists of five chapters. It is intended to trace a single connecting thread by providing in the first four chapters a look at key topics that define a student's undergraduate experience. These topics are also stages of a student's trajectory through four years of undergraduate life and into postgraduate programs. The fifth chapter explores the experience of students enrolled in graduate programs and those who elect a combined undergraduate and graduate degree path. Illustrated by cases and examples from member institutions, this staged journey reveals in some detail the dimensions and unique qualities of a distinctive kind of American higher education. (The following member institutions are not included in these examples; some joined the consortium after the book's completion: California Lutheran University, Hampton University, Roger Williams University, and University of New Haven.)

The book also weaves the NAC&U examples into a pattern by placing them within the context of higher education research relevant to each of the topics. Through this discussion, we seek to understand not only the core features of the education the NAC&U consortium aspires to make available but also essential elements of a model that can achieve the expansive goals of a distinctively American undergraduate education.

Chapter 1 provides an overview of what is distinctive about the NAC&U model. Starting with the founders' vision, the chapter presents instances of the model's distinctive definition of the *college experience* through examples of what it means to integrate liberal arts, professional studies, and civic responsibility.

The evidence for the economic value of a college degree is clear and compelling. This chapter reports findings from national surveys of employers that show how the abilities sought by today's employers closely match the goals of undergraduate learning. The specific value proposition of the NAC&U consortium is that these goals can be achieved most effectively through courses of study that enable students to link knowledge to the development of professional skills with a commitment to civic engagement. This strategy is supported by research that shows that the exploration of meaning and purpose enables students to connect their college learning with preparation for the future in fruitful ways.

Chapter 2 focuses on integrated learning practices that bring together liberal learning and professional preparation. It provides cases of high-impact practices, including experiential learning, that unfold through dynamic connections between classrooms and the wider world, as experienced by students and faculty.

This chapter places NAC&U's quest for more integrated teaching and learning within the context of research that shows how certain educational practices have a particularly high impact in advancing student learning. The articulation of clear learning goals, effective modeling of what is to be learned, active practice of these things, and feedback on performance turn out to be the basis for developing expertise in all fields. These are the heart of effective education.

Chapter 3 examines the impact of intentional campus community life on students' journeys toward adult identity. It emphasizes student experiences that reveal life on NAC&U campuses as a tapestry of personal, social, academic, and vocational growth that is deeply satisfying as well as challenging and, in many instances, transformative.

This chapter presents evidence for the key role that human relationships and social involvement with professors and peers plays in student success in college. A high-quality community life on campus provides the necessary soil for students to flourish, just as Ernest Boyer and the founders of the NAC&U understood. Effective undergraduate education, in other words, depends on a campus climate of respect, inclusion, and trust in which academic expectations are high and supported by intentional design.

This chapter also explains how various NAC&U campus programs enable students to explore future career possibilities. It describes how externships and placements work, illustrating the kind of productive alignments between academic learning, including choice of major programs, and exploration of professional and service experiences that students find especially valuable.

American higher education has a long history of linking campus learning with experience in various other sectors of society. Recently, concerns about preparing students for a more competitive economic environment have spurred experimentation with new ways of facilitating students' exploration of future career possibilities, seeking more effective ways to achieve these ends. This chapter describes the core features of these emerging models that help students connect their developing academic abilities to the demands of the world of work.

Chapter 4 emphasizes how NAC&U campuses enable students to integrate their learning with career preparation and personal development within the wider perspectives of service to others through citizenship in the community, profession, nation, and world. Examples range from environmental studies and study abroad to service experiences, campus-community partnerships, and civic and political engagement as schools for citizenship.

This focus on civic responsibility has deep roots in American higher education. The charters of many colleges and universities, public and private, state that the education of citizens is an essential, defining purpose of higher education in the United States. This chapter examines contemporary efforts to rearticulate and express that tradition in ways suited to today's students and social context. It shows how civic responsibility can function as one of the most powerful means of fostering the growth of purpose in young lives by providing content to the search for aims that engage and fulfill the self while also integrating people into relationships and goals that transcend the individual.

In Chapter 5 the key theme of integrated learning is shown in the distinctive ways NAC&U campus officials have organized their graduate programs. With a focus on enabling students who are already pursuing professional work to advance their careers, this chapter profiles a number of graduate professional programs that bring liberal learning and civic perspectives into the preparation of professionals in various areas of study, from business and engineering to the health fields, social work, and journalism. A number of these programs feature joint degree programs that enable undergraduates to advance to a professional degree in less time and with fewer obstacles while remaining in the NAC&U environment of challenging learning and a supportive campus culture oriented toward service to the larger civic community.

The conclusion returns to the opening themes, restating the distinctive features of an NAC&U education while situating them in relation to what is known about how best to make college a time of personal growth and intellectual development. In doing so, this section summarizes and articulates the following elements of this model of undergraduate education that could provide important direction for the improvement of higher education as a whole:

1. Courses of study that integrate the broad aims of the liberal arts, development of professional competence, and a sense of civic responsibility
2. Practices of teaching and learning that engage and promote student learning through employment of high-impact practices tested by research
3. Campus community climate characterized by inclusive yet demanding expectations shared among students and faculty that support healthy relationships and personal growth
4. Cultivation of relationships between campus and the larger community and world to support educational experiences that enhance students' professional and career developments as well as their commitment to civic partnership and service to the world

The NAC&U campuses described in this book do not fully exemplify this ideal model—no actual college could. Each of the book's chapters explore examples of how these campuses are currently pursuing such a model seriously and imaginatively. One purpose of this book is to enable NAC&U administrators to recognize more clearly their common endeavor as well as their distinctive strengths. The voices of students and faculty will make clear how an NAC&U education can set a purposeful path toward a rewarding college experience and beyond, to a life that is really worth living.

Enjoy the journey!

I

THE NEW AMERICAN COLLEGES AND UNIVERSITIES EXPERIENCE

Integrating Liberal Arts, Professional Studies, and Civic Responsibility

For today's young Americans and their parents, deciding whether to attend college is one of the most important decisions they will ever make. There are good, practical reasons for students and their parents to take pains to make going to college possible. Having a college degree has profound effects on one's economic well-being, especially over a lifetime.[1] In a nationwide survey, major employers were asked what graduates need to succeed in today's economy. More than 90% said that in addition to career-specific skills, they sought new employees who had a broad range of knowledge about the world and a strong sense of social responsibility.

This national sample of employers emphasized they were seeking college graduates who could do more than fill the requirements for their first job. The employers surveyed said their companies needed employees who could solve complex problems of many kinds, analyze information and situations, and communicate effectively; too often, it seemed, their new hires lacked one or more of these abilities. The employers believed that a good college education could and should develop these abilities, which are also the traditional aims of what is called education in the liberal arts.

The research project concluded that the challenges of the twenty-first century demand that today's young people develop four areas of competence that coincide closely with the abilities employers are seeking. First, students need to gain knowledge of human cultures as well as of the physical and natural world. Second, they must be able to think well, meaning they have

7

the ability to inquire and analyze information, think critically and creatively, communicate well in speech and writing, understand quantitative reasoning, use information technology competently, and be able to solve problems with others. Third, students need to grow in personal and social responsibility, including the competence to take part in public affairs and to learn over a lifetime. Fourth, they must be able to integrate their learning to make sense of the world and be able to apply it.[2]

By fostering these capacities in students, colleges and universities are providing an extremely valuable service. Going to college, then, by any measure, turns out to be a very cost-effective investment. At the same time, college is expensive. Students and their parents rightly ask whether they are getting a high enough value from this investment of time and money. They want to be confident that pursuing a path of study and attending a particular institution will provide all a college education should.

But economic advantage is only the beginning of the value that going to college offers. Other values are in some ways even more practically important than the economic payoff, and these other effects of a good college education are more long lasting and profound. College changes lives. It enables young people to grow into adulthood ready to face the world. But college also changes the society and the world. It is the indispensable provider of key skills that power the economy, especially in this era of information-driven innovation. But equally important, by fostering the growth of students' interests and self-knowledge, a college education also nurtures new generations of citizens who can explore, create, and contribute in unique ways to make their nation and the world better.

How, then, do you get the most out of college? What should your strategy be for making the big investment of time and money really worthwhile? Getting the most out of a college experience requires active engagement on the part of the students themselves. Colleges can make this all-important personal engagement more likely and more valuable for individual students by providing the right context for them to flourish.

Considerable evidence shows that situations in which students are encouraged to relate what they learn to actual experience are especially effective in making it possible to acquire the four capacities previously noted. Likewise, learning happens more efficiently when students are given opportunities to apply what they study in the classroom to analyzing and solving problems in the world beyond the classroom. Having a chance to consider and address big questions about the world and about one's own life stimulates the imagination and expands the mind and sympathies, as does developing relationships with diverse kinds of students, staff, and people outside the campus. It is important for standards of performance to be high, and at the same time for students to receive support and encouragement in meeting these standards. These approaches are often called *high-impact* teaching practices because of their demonstrated ability to motivate students to take advantage of and get the most out of the opportunities college offers.[3]

Furthermore, the benefits of these high-impact practices are all magnified when they take place in a campus climate that emphasizes and supports personal relationships between students and faculty and among students. Such relationships are part of a campus climate that research indicates is especially favorable to learning and self-development among students.[4] Students are best able to learn about themselves and what their gifts are in such environments. By discovering what really interests them, opening their minds to previously unknown possibilities, and developing new capacities through self-discipline and hard work, they are able to bring all this together to forge a purpose for living that will promote their growth in ways that connect with others and better the world.[5]

To realize your potential it is important for you to find the right fit between the type of college and the kind of person you wish to become. What are your aspirations for your future? What are the ideals that truly motivate you? What sort of environment will most help you make the most of your gifts and enable you to grow through significant relationships with peers and mentors? In this book, I invite you to take a serious look from many angles at a distinctive kind of college experience, a brand if you will: the 25 private colleges and universities that constitute the New American Colleges and Universities (NAC&U).

Introducing the NAC&U

The NAC&U consortium comprises 25 institutions: Arcadia University, Belmont University, California Lutheran University, Drury University, Hamline University, Hampton University, John Carroll University, Manhattan College, Nazareth College, North Central College, Ohio Northern University, Pacific Lutheran University, Roger Williams University, Samford University, St. Edward's University, The Sage Colleges, University of Scranton, University of Evansville, University of La Verne, University of New Haven, University of Redlands, Valparaiso University, Wagner College, Westminster College, and Widener University.

These institutions are each quite distinct in their mission, faculty, and student body. NAC&U institutions are geographically distributed across the United States, but they all have a common goal: to provide a distinctive educational experience, described as "dedicated to the purposeful integration of liberal education, professional studies, and civic engagement." All of them provide this kind of education in primarily residential settings in small to middle-size campus communities of between 2,000 and 7,500 students. At NAC&U institutions, faculty and staff all see themselves as educators sharing a calling to foster their students' growth as people and as citizens. They are regularly cited as among the colleges that provide the best value for the money as well as a diverse array of areas of study, a strong campus community, and ways to join academic preparation to career preparation.

In other words, an NAC&U education is intended to enable students to discover and develop your talents so you can make a place for yourself in the world in an important way that includes finding work and a satisfying career. Additionally, an NAC&U education aims to equip you to learn for a lifetime, enabling you to make sense of today's fast-changing and often confusing world. Even more, an NAC&U education is integrative by design, providing the breadth and depth of vision necessary for you to find what you want to stand for in life and hone your specific talents to contribute positively to your nation and the world.

To understand the kind of educational experience these institutions try to provide, it helps to understand something of the background of the organization and its animating spirit.

What NAC&U Stands For

As in all great ventures, this one began with a vision, but it was a vision of what was possible rather than a utopia. In the 1990s there was increasing concern that American higher education was giving up on its most distinctive heritage; that is, that college could and should teach students how to learn about the world and then apply that learning to the betterment of their own lives and those around them. To address this concern, a group of leaders in higher education gathered at Wingspread, the visionary house in Wisconsin designed by the great architect Frank Lloyd Wright. The group included Alexander Astin, who had written extensively on what American students aspired to in their education and their futures; Ernest Boyer, distinguished president of the Carnegie Foundation for the Advancement of Teaching, who contributed his broad overview of higher education as a whole; and Frank Wong, vice president of the University of Redlands, one of today's NAC&U members. These leaders proposed a renewal of the ideal of what they called the *New American College*, which they defined as an institution of higher learning dedicated to the integration rather than the specialized separation of research and teaching, theory and practice, and learning and life.[6]

That meeting in 1995 produced the Association of New American Colleges, which subsequently became the NAC&U. The organization continues to stand for its founding vision of creating an integrative higher education reflected in the motto that declares its mission: "the purposeful integration of liberal education, professional studies, and civic engagement." This mission is a demanding one; it requires the member institutions to strive actively for an educational ideal that resists the drift toward specialization and separation that is such a marked feature of contemporary life. Instead, NAC&U as a consortium and its members as particular institutions work actively to embody their alternative vision of a new American college. Boyer described that aim well by insisting that to achieve it "all parts of campus life—recruitment, orientation, curriculum, teaching, residence hall living, and the rest—must relate to one another and contribute to a sense of wholeness." Boyer singled out the idea of community to describe this aim:

> We emphasize this commitment to community not out of a sentimental attachment to tradition, but because our democratic way of life and perhaps our survival as a people rest on whether we can move beyond self-interest and begin to understand better the realities of our dependence on each other.[7]

An NAC&U education takes place on campuses designed to foster the kind of community spirit Boyer urged. All 25 member colleges and universities are places where education is personal, and faculty see themselves as scholar teachers devoted to developing their students' capacities to take part in the life of the mind. They know their students personally and interact with them frequently. In the same way, students often remark on finding a welcoming sense of community, whether they reside on campus or commute.

Because of the intimate scale of NAC&U campuses, academic work easily blends with an array of extracurricular activities, ranging from sports to the performing and visual arts. These are not impersonal institutions; people know faces and names, and students and staff find it natural to look out for one another. Students typically find it easy to develop relationships with career counselors who can help them connect their academic interests with professional preparation, and students need not enter their final year without vocational direction or options. Additionally, NAC&U institutions encourage students to become involved with communities beyond the campus. Civic engagement is a prominent feature of curricular and extracurricular student life. In this book, you will get to know a good deal about the common aspects of an NAC&U education and the distinctive features of the various member campuses that tend to support the judgment of Edward

L. Ayers, historian and president emeritus of the University of Richmond: "NAC&U lives up to Boyer's vision better than any other organization in higher education."[8]

These characteristics are directly related to the aim of this distinctive brand of education: integrating liberal arts, professional studies, and civic responsibility. The faculty and staff of all the institutional members of the NAC&U consortium work hard to maintain a certain type of campus climate that enables students to thrive through making connections to their personal goals, experience the excitement of exploring knowledge, prepare for a career, and learn how to be an active citizen.

A Kaleidoscope of the NAC&U Experience

To get a sense of what integrating liberal arts, professional studies, and civic responsibility looks like at some of these campuses, let's consider each of these three elements and how various campuses make them work together.

The Power of Liberal Learning

All NAC&U campuses place emphasis on enabling their students to know themselves and their abilities as well as providing them with opportunities to develop a sophisticated understanding of the world. To achieve these goals, the academic programs focus on developing students' intellectual and practical skills, such as analytical ability, problem solving, facility in written and spoken communication, and an appreciation for human diversity and creativity, all of which have been traditionally identified as the goals of a liberal arts education. This typically means studying a variety of subjects and intellectual disciplines to better understand the complex world we inhabit. Often, these subjects are divided into three groups: mathematics and the natural sciences, which focus on how the world works and how to devise new technologies to work on the world; the social sciences, which aim to understand the way human society and human beings work; and the arts and humanities, which explore what it is like to be human and how to take part in the human world. It is worth noting that the capacities developed by liberal learning are the same ones identified in the previously mentioned national employer survey as those that give job seekers an edge.[9]

A strong grounding in the liberal arts, which is a core mission of all NAC&U institutions, can produce amazing results. Liberal learning enables people to see farther, understand more deeply, and grasp problems more effectively than would be possible without such training by giving students ways to notice what most do not; see in new ways; analyze how nature works and how we have come to live and think as we do; and investigate the values and beliefs that guide societies and individuals, especially when these influences are unnoticed. Using these techniques can provide levers to change seemingly impossible problems or move obstacles.

For example, everyone must cope with the side effects of today's technology. These can be serious, as when the environmental effects of industrial processes challenge the quality of life. Many find these types of negative effects confusing, so they shy away from confronting such problems until they become serious or even overwhelming threats perhaps to their families and communities. The virtue of liberal learning, as we will see shortly, is that it can change mind-sets by enabling people to learn how to think more flexibly and broadly so they can work with various, sometimes opposing, points of view and not be overwhelmed by the conflict. Liberally educated people can confidently expect to grasp complex problems and work with others to solve them. But it takes time and effort to acquire these abilities, which is what college education in the liberal arts is for.

Learning Communities at Wagner College

At Wagner College, on New York City's Staten Island, first-year students begin their college careers with a vivid introduction to these elements of liberal learning. All new Wagner students become part of the Wagner Plan for the Practical Liberal Arts, the plan of study shared by all Wagner students, called a *learning community*. Each learning community consists of two groups of 14 students led by two faculty members who teach two courses in their disciplines that are linked by a common theme or topic. As part of these courses, students spend about three hours per week in off-campus activities ranging from field trips to New York metropolitan sites to service-learning with community organizations. Along with the two linked courses, the third component of the Wagner learning community is the reflective tutorial in which students analyze intensively, discuss, and write about the connections between the concepts in their classes and their experiences off campus. The small class size is designed to encourage personal interactions among students and faculty. The fact that two courses from different disciplines are linked allows faculty members from different departments to interact with each other as well as with the students.

In the first-year learning community, Living on Spaceship Earth, students focus on a big question: Given how tightly living things and technologies are interconnected in the planetary environment, how is it possible to sustain economic vitality and a positive environment for the complex web of living things? To understand this question, they study biology, learning about the world of organisms and their environments, and economics, where they discover and learn to use intellectual tools for analyzing how businesses, jobs, and incomes connect with each other. In Living on Spaceship Earth, the biology course, taught by Donald Stearns, chair of the biology department, and the economics course, taught by a professor in the economics department, are linked by a reflective tutorial taught by a member of the English department. The tutorial provides continual instruction and practice with the critical skills of written and oral communication, using the questions introduced throughout the activities of the learning community as the common theme.

But all this is not simply an academic exercise. The field component of the experience is a real problem in the real world. For five consecutive Fridays, all 28 students and both professors spend a full day in Toms River, New Jersey, which is not far from the Wagner campus. This town has abnormal levels of adolescent and child cancers, thought to be the result of chemical dumping in a nearby landfill. Under present law, the dumping is entirely legal. On those Friday visits, students and faculty meet with the families affected, elected officials, local media, and then with state and federal Environmental Protection Agency officials in New Jersey and Manhattan to understand the various dimensions of the problem. They attend town meetings to learn how local citizens are thinking about responding to it. Through all this, their assignment is to do serious research toward answering perplexing, real-world questions of concern to Toms River residents: How would a scientifically trained investigator know if the elevated cancer rates are traceable to chemical dumping? and How would a social scientist understand the economic impact of these events on the community of Toms River?

To complete these demanding assignments, students, guided by their professors, write research papers on specific aspects of these issues. In the process, they discover through their own experience what they need to learn as well as the intellectual and communications skills they must develop to figure out the situation and work with others to resolve the problem. They are also learning that Wagner will provide the means to develop their abilities to learn and perform as adults. The professors will remain students' academic advisers until they declare a major field of study, providing continuity between this first experience of academic investigation and what will come later in their college careers. At the end of the semester, the students participate in a poster session in which they present their work to the other learning communities (pursuing different topics and questions) as well as to invited members of the Toms River community and local media. Thus, they must take public responsibility for their learning.

This is liberal learning in action. Although few of these students will choose biology, economics, or business as majors, they will all live in communities that will face environmental challenges, and as citizens, they will all vote. The experience of the learning community, which is reinforced by each of the students' four years in additional learning communities on different questions examined by different disciplines, reveals further questions that are important to understand. Why do people, not only as individuals but also in organizations, do what they do? How does technology interact with natural and social processes? What values do and ought to guide these interactions? Through their experience in these courses, the students not only gained knowledge and skill but also began to acquire the confidence of thinking for themselves and being able to have an impact on the world. These are the great gains made possible by liberal education.

Mastering New Worlds of Information at Valparaiso University
When asked about his experience with the general studies curriculum, a graduating senior at Valparaiso singled out one of the courses for its relevance:

> Until I took Information Research Strategies I never really knew how to research properly. . . . This course is good for fine-tuning my research skills, and I see some of my friends who haven't taken it struggling. Research is hard; it's more than a Google search. That's why this course is beneficial.

We have seen how important research skills were for the students in the Living on Spaceship Earth learning community at Wagner College. At Valparaiso, students evidently come to the same conclusion, thanks to their experience with Information Research Strategies, a course taught by the library and information sciences department and part of Valparaiso's general studies curriculum. This set of courses for all students is intended to improve their ability to analyze and solve problems, communicate effectively, and employ their academic knowledge in real-world situations. The general studies curriculum is a good example of the kind of liberal learning an NAC&U education provides that can be so valuable.

As with other courses in general studies, Information Research Strategies is organized around some key features of high-impact learning. It is open to all students and is designed to provide them with a common core of knowledge and skill to interact in the online world. Students report that they find this course highly relevant. It gives them clear goals for directing their efforts. Through the instructor's approach, it provides students with living models of the knowledge to be mastered and how to use and apply that knowledge. Most important, it also provides feedback and coaching so students can practice and improve their competence in the skills they are trying to learn.

Through clearly outlined goals, students can see what they are expected to learn and can monitor how well they are succeeding in their learning. But this is also a blended, or hybrid, course, meaning that it is partly taught online and partly in person. Students are expected to do their reading in advance of class sessions. They are frequently quizzed about what they have read, which is another demonstrated aid to effective learning, and they use a number of online tools such as video tutorials, podcasts, and online discussions to prepare for class meetings that are lively and highly interactive.

Students are assigned to research an emerging technology and must create a research log and an annotated bibliography to document how they go about their searching. They then work together in groups to define various strategies for research. The course culminates with student groups grappling with real-life case studies. This course also increases students' engagement with their learning by providing opportunities to apply their new skills to contexts that are challenging and clearly important. With assistance from the instructor, the students document their problem-solving strategies and present the results for general critique and discussion.

Students' experience with this course makes clear to them that their level of knowledge and skill have grown significantly, illustrated by the Valparaiso student's comments on page 15. By learning how to create systematic research strategies, students were also developing critical thinking skills that would enhance not only their college success but also their future. They were starting to develop lifelong habits of learning that would serve them in good stead when confronted with the vast amounts of information likely to be typical in their future. They left the course able to analyze a variety of information formats and decide for themselves how best to access and use these sources in a variety of contexts.

These are all very valuable skills to list on any job résumé. But as part of their liberal education at Valparaiso, students also became accustomed to recognizing that using information has social, legal, and ethical implications. Such an understanding will set these students apart from others less sensitive to the far-reaching significance of today's emerging technologies. That will undoubtedly prove useful to them in their future careers, but it will also enhance their lives as mature and responsible citizens.[10]

Student Research at Samford University

"You go through high school thinking your teachers know all the answers," said Walter Turner, an African American sophomore chemistry major at Samford University in Birmingham, Alabama. "In college," he continued, "your professors help you find answers to new questions." Walter spent the previous summer investigating the ability of fungi that grow wild on the trunks of felled trees to remove harmful molecules from water such as those left from drugs that contaminate water supplies. This is an interesting scientific problem that also has important practice implications. As Walter pointed out, providing clean and safe water is going to get harder in this century. "I hope this project can make some small contribution to reaching that goal."

Walter spent the summer working closely with two professors in the Department of Chemistry and Biochemistry at Samford—Denise Gregory and Lisa Nagy. The faculty were indeed stimulating Walter to find answers to new questions about how the physical world works. His project is part of the way Samford enhances its students' learning and accelerates their careers through student-faculty research. This is another advantage of the size and highly personal atmosphere of NAC&U institutions; it makes joining with faculty in cutting-edge research part of the regular academic program rather than just something to read about.

Walter's project also illustrates how deep involvement in an area of study can open up new questions and lead to making connections that were at first invisible. In Walter's case, it turned out that getting the chemistry right, finding the right mushrooms that could detoxify water, involved more than learning to identify particular species of fungi and then growing them in the laboratory. Walter discovered he had to expand his understanding of biochemistry by learning some biology, specifically modern genetics.

Walter's student-faculty research team consisted of three other students, the two faculty mentors, and himself. Together they spent time identifying the enzymes that bonded with and changed the chemical structure of particular drugs found in local water. Once it became clear which enzymes neutralized harmful molecules in the drugs, they then had to figure out how to determine which species of mushroom produced those enzymes. The team then spent weeks growing mushrooms to test their hypothesis that these fungi can change the chemical structure of the drugs and clean up contaminated water sources. Their map of the chemical processes that underlie these effects will be their contribution to science and the health of the local environment.

An advantage of taking part in student-faculty research for students like Walter is that it gives them an inside look at faculty work. In addition to the lab work and reading the literature, these students join the full department faculty once a week in a departmental colloquium. In this setting, members of the department present their research for critique and discussion in the time-honored procedure by which the sciences advance knowledge. Students observe experts interacting with each other and eventually present their own work as novice researchers.

This has changed Walter's career plans as well. He began Samford intending to become a pharmacist, but, after his summer of student-faculty research, he is now seriously considering graduate programs in chemistry. His experience at Samford is not unusual. By delving deeply into an area of intellectual interest, an activity provided by a liberal arts environment, Walter ended up connecting the needs of the communities of his home state with the possibility of a meaningful career in a cutting-edge industry.[11]

Integrating Professional Studies

All NAC&U institutions put a great deal of effort into providing their students with state-of-the-art preparation for professional life and occupational success in diverse fields. Different campuses provide a wide variety of professional majors in fields ranging from science and technology (e.g., engineering and computer science) to business, human services (e.g., education, nursing, premedicine, and prelaw), architecture, and the performing and visual arts. In these courses of study, students begin to shape their future careers. Some of these programs and how they work are presented in Chapters 2 and 3. But it is important to realize that an NAC&U education provides a whole variety of ways to connect college learning with future careers. Through various forms of innovative internships and involvements in the worlds of work and professional practice, students in a variety of majors, not just the professional programs, learn by doing as well as by classroom instruction.

The unique aspect of an NAC&U education is the close relationship between professional majors and liberal learning. As we have seen, the aim of this integration is to ensure that students in whatever field develop the four core competencies employers want from the graduates they hire: knowledge of the physical world and human cultures, the ability to think critically and broadly, growth in personal and social responsibility, and an integrated understanding that manifests itself in applying knowledge to life. The intention behind integrating professional majors with liberal arts perspectives is to encourage students' ethical integrity, ability to work well with diverse colleagues, concern with contributing to the larger community, and interest in continued learning.

Not all students arrive at college with a clear career trajectory. Many are unsure what to major in and unclear about how particular majors might lead to various careers after graduation. One of the benefits of enrolling in a liberal arts curriculum is that it allows and encourages students to explore ideas and the world. For such students, an NAC&U education is especially valuable. In addition to having the chance to explore, they have a lot of support for turning their exploration into a specific future career.

From Academic Major to a Career at the University of Redlands

Consider the experience of Darrell Rice, a senior psychology major at the University of Redlands in Southern California. Darrell's professor in his abnormal psychology course, Celine Ko, encouraged him to complement his classroom learning with exposure to clinical populations and different mental health issues that had been topics of discussion in the class. As part of their capstone experience at Redlands, seniors in every major must engage in a field experience that is closely tied to their major area of concentration. After consulting further with his professor, Darrell chose the Riverside Free Clinic, a teaching clinic staffed collaboratively by medical and graduate students from the University of California at Riverside and the University of California, Los Angeles, along with a number of other health professions. The clinic serves vulnerable populations who seek assistance through a walk-in health program and operate the longtime soup kitchen outreach, Project FOOD, at the historic First Congregational Church. Paul Lyons of Riverside's School of Medicine oversees the clinic and its projects.

Darrell and other undergraduate volunteers from the University of Redlands had the opportunity to practice the skills they were learning in their courses while observing the practical meaning of the counseling, medical, social justice, and advocacy concepts and theories they were discussing in the classroom. For 10 hours each week, Darrell's clinic assignment entailed providing assistance and support to the graduate students who managed the logistics of the clinic. He also observed clinical psychology graduate students providing counseling support and working with the medical staff to provide an integrated care environment to improve the lives of an underserved, low-income population. These experiences provided the basis for the report and research papers he developed as part of his senior capstone course in psychology.

Darrell's response was enthusiastic. "I had an amazing experience at the clinic! At first glance, the clinic seems like pure chaos but the longer I was there the more I realized how organized and efficient it was," he reported. "I was able to sit in on a counseling/smoking cessation session. It is one thing," he said, "to learn about therapy or counseling in an abnormal psychology class or counseling class. It is another thing entirely to see it firsthand."

Along with his classmates, Darrell experienced direct, supervised contact with clients. He was able to shadow and observe clinical psychologists and graduate students at work in a live, real practice setting. Moreover, the placement enabled him to observe and take part in collaborative health care treatment planning and interventions based on an approach that sought to integrate the biological with the psychological in treating clients. The

Redlands seniors also learned the basics of the management side of a free-standing clinic. So the students gained a deeper sense of what it is like to be a clinical psychologist than they would have had they remained in the academic setting alone. This combination of theoretical training and practical experience is the great strength of many professional majors at Redlands, as at other NAC&U campuses.

Darrell confirmed that his experience at the Riverside Free Clinic provided him with invaluable insight into issues related to mental health disorders. He also reported that his experience at the clinic was very important for solidifying his decision to apply to a PhD program in clinical psychology. From the clinic experience, he gained a new perspective and a strong commitment to pursue a career in clinical psychology to serve older adults, which is a growing sector of the American population in great need of the services of an able psychologist.[12]

The benefits of internships and placements such as Darrell Rice experienced at Redlands are complemented by campus programs that provide students with a number of resources for connecting their academic learning with jobs and careers. Every NAC&U campus has career counselors who provide guidance on how to word the job-relevant skills students have learned in academic courses on their résumés for potential employers as well as how to interview effectively. In addition, these programs organize on-campus visits by recruiters from many employers at career fairs where students can learn about the jobs that are available and their requirements, meet prospective employers in a friendly setting, and leave résumés with recruiters. Opportunities for résumé preparation with faculty and career counselors are among the services that NAC&U campuses provide for making the transition from college to a first job.

Alumni as Career Coaches at Manhattan College

Every year 150 seniors are accepted to the Alumni Connection Career Services program from all five Manhattan College schools with majors ranging from engineering to the liberal arts. Located in the New York City borough of the Bronx, Manhattan College is able to bring to campus representatives from employers in a wide area around the city. Participating students are matched with an alumnus or alumna of the college who had the same major and career interests, thus creating support from the beginning. Students also attend a mandatory workshop run by the career counseling center to learn what will be expected of them and where they will be meeting their alumni mentors and to hear advice from former mentors. Over two semesters, students then meet regularly with their mentors as they work on their career plans, concretely explore possible career paths, practice interviewing skills, and then begin interviewing for jobs. At the end of the spring semester, all join in a celebratory mentor dinner. The results are impressive. According to Manhattan's graduating senior survey, student participants in the program report a 73% success rate in securing employment by graduation.

The connections and personal relationships the program makes possible for students and mentors are valuable even, and perhaps especially, for students who start out thinking they already know where they are headed. Joseph, who is a graduate in the investment banking business, reported how he realized that his protégé Julie, while intent on a traditional investment banking career, had skills and the personality that might be better suited to other areas of the finance industry. Joe counseled Julie to widen her search and made introductions that resulted in Julie's securing a competitive internship with a wealth management company, which turned into an employment offer after graduation. Julie is thriving as a financial adviser, and she and Joseph believe she has landed in the right place for career growth and high job satisfaction.

Such relationships between mentors and protégés often last beyond the Alumni Connection Career Services program. Graduates of the program often return as mentors after a few years in their careers, as was the case with Joseph when he began his work with Julie. Mentors can influence their companies' hiring decisions in favor of the program's participants, work with their protégé to improve their résumés, make introductions to hiring managers, and have candid conversations with their protégé about future prospects and strategy. As returning graduates, they do this because they themselves received help from the program.

Mentors can also play an important role in helping students understand the value of integrating the various parts of their college learning. Frank, who mentors engineering students, takes his protégés on site visits to potential employers. He notes that "one of the biggest insights that his mentees often cite" is recognizing "the importance for career success in engineering of leadership skills, learned mostly from involvement in campus and civic activities, in addition to technical expertise." The relationships between mentors and protégé can also extend well beyond the first job. For example, when considering whether to accept an offer to move to a Fortune 500 company, a former protégé credited his former mentor with advising him to consider his long-term life purposes as well as his short-term career goals. Besides its practical benefits to students, this program makes it possible for Manhattan alumni to give back to their alma mater in a personal and rewarding way, and that they want to do so testifies to the robust campus ethic of mutual support among students and staff. In the process, they share directly in ,the educational mission of the college, proving its concern for its students' growth as professionals and as people beyond graduation.[13]

Integrating Civic Responsibility

Another important element of an NAC&U education is fostering civic responsibility among students. NAC&U administrators deliberately strive to maintain a campus climate in which everyone—students, faculty, and staff—is expected to treat each other with fairness and respect. They are also expected to recognize the contributions of others and be willing to give as well as receive assistance and recognition, all qualities of the alumni mentoring program previously discussed. In this case, the whole really is greater than the sum of the parts. And NAC&U campuses are noteworthy for the degree to which they embody a spirit of mutual care. But this civic spirit is not confined to the campus. In study abroad programs and a range of internship and service opportunities, these colleges support their students in finding unique and effective ways to contribute to the larger life of their world.

Learning, Leadership, Service at John Carroll University
On its campus in Cleveland, Ohio, John Carroll University gives practical expression to its defining mission, which it sums up as "Learning, Leadership, Service," grounded in the institution's "Catholic and Jesuit Identity." Everyone at John Carroll is very proud of its distinctive approach to integrating students' experience by providing a nourishing atmosphere for the whole student.

John Carroll University gives special attention to connecting students' first experiences of the institution to the overarching goals of engagement with learning. Such experiences at the beginning of college are among the most important for students' overall development, setting enduring expectations of what higher education is for and what the coming years will be about. It is noteworthy that John Carroll leaders foreground the idea of what they call "vocational discernment." Before they begin their first semester, students, along with their parents, take part in two days of introduction to the values embodied in the university's programs. In groups of 100, students encounter an approach to decision making that encapsulates John Carroll's educational mission. Students are asked to reflect on three questions: Who am I and what am I passionate about? Where am I needed in the world? and How am I going to get there? While students are not expected to have ready or complete answers to these leading questions, they are asked to take them back home, discuss them with their parents and friends, and think about them.

This orientation workshop is the first step students take toward addressing John Carroll's first two integrating learning goals: "understanding and valuing their own socio-cultural identities" and "articulating their own goals, values, and skills." These learning goals continue to surface throughout the students' four years, reinforced by a number of programs and activities intentionally organized to keep bringing students back to these fundamental themes. The first major reinforcement occurs right away, during a five-day orientation program called Streak Week. On one of those days, called Living the Mission Day, entering students experience for themselves the university's core mission of learning, leadership, and service in ways structured by its Catholic and Jesuit ethos.

On Living the Mission Day, students must choose among four experiences. For the first option, students may take part in the Cleveland Neighborhood Project, a service experience that connects them with new classmates and some of the university's urban neighbors with whom they may later develop relationships through various community partner organizations. For the second option, students may spend the day on an outdoor retreat run by the campus ministry office, learning about the university's mission, reflecting further on their initial vocational questions, and building personal connections with their classmates and upper-class facilitators. For the third option, students may take a bus tour, guided by faculty and upper-class students, to several of Cleveland's outstanding cultural institutions, gaining an introduction to some of the city's ethnic and religious diversity. For the fourth option, called Leadership, students work in small groups to accomplish tasks. Led by upper-class facilitators, these groups are designed to provide entering students with insight about what is needed for teamwork and leadership through group and individual reflection with fellow students interested in the same issues.

Student response to Living the Mission Day is heavily positive. "While I was working on the Cleveland Neighborhood Project," reported one freshman, "I was able to meet some other new students and actually see how I could make a difference in the neighborhood, motivating me to do more [of this] while I am a student at John Carroll." The faith-oriented retreat also makes an important impact on participants. One Roman Catholic student had never before taken part in a retreat, and the experience started him on some new paths. "I met some of my closest friends on this retreat," he noted, "and I was able to become connected to the Campus Ministry department as well." The study tour to Severance Hall, the Cleveland Museum of Art, the Maltz Museum of Jewish Heritage, and other sites also seems to spark ongoing and varied involvements. "I'll never walk by a painting anywhere again," exclaimed a student, "without thinking about that day."

In addition to a large number of service-learning courses available in the curriculum as well as involvement in community partnerships in which some of the beginning students participated, John Carroll provides a number of programs for students to continue to pursue those initial questions about vocation in contexts that match their growing personal answers to questions of identity, values, and how they can shape their lives to respond to the needs of the world, local and distant. For example, the university provides a prehealth studies program, a very popular one, thanks to the institution's long-standing reputation for preparing students for careers in health fields, that goes beyond the expected rigorous science curriculum. Participating students join their peers in community service and social justice projects that have meaning for the health professions. It also provides students with career counseling from the prehealth advising office that houses a physician in residence as well as full-time advisory personnel. Advice about medical or dental school applications or careers in physical therapy or pharmacy, for instance, is also attuned to the university's concern with how its central values of learning, leadership, and service can be lived in the health fields.

Students who come to John Carroll with a strong concern for social justice and the public sphere can apply for the Arrupe Scholars Program, a comprehensive scholarship that supports a cohort of students each year who commit to four years of social justice work that includes community service; advocacy for the most vulnerable; and organized reflection on identity, purpose, and vocation. During each year of the program, Arrupe Scholars act and reflect. In addition to their service and social justice work, these students also take a seminar each year that ties their experiences to academic learning through investigation and research. They study the causes of injustice and its processes in ways that support human solidarity.

During the program, students work on an e-portfolio that documents their curricular and cocurricular learning about social justice and advocacy. The program contributes strong leaders to campus culture who often organize and sponsor campuswide events to focus attention on social needs and world crises. It also enables participants to develop as critical thinkers and agents of social improvement in areas they feel particularly drawn to.[14]

Service Abroad at Belmont University

At Belmont University in Nashville, Tennessee, a service trip abroad took students' creativity in directions no one had foreseen. Committed students were able to set in motion whole new programs. The personal scale of Belmont, whose student body numbers a few thousand rather than tens of thousands, makes possible faculty responsiveness to student initiatives and needs that might get lost in larger institutions.

Belmont has a strong tradition of globally focused education. The institution has a long history, rooted in its Christian identity, of sponsoring student service trips in the United States and abroad. Through such experiences of service, two successful graduates, Peter and Gracie Rosenberger, began a philanthropic program several years ago called Standing With Hope to provide prosthetic limbs for residents of Ghana in West Africa. The philanthropy had no direct connection with the university until a student saw an opportunity and took the initiative to create a new program, enlisting fellow students and Belmont faculty in the process.

After returning to campus from a university-sponsored service trip to Ghana, this student, majoring in physical therapy, found herself stirred by the idea of a new transnational collaboration. Belmont was already connected with a fledgling physical therapy program at the University of Ghana in Accra. This student proposed developing a program in which Belmont students and University of Accra physical therapy students would work together to provide assistance to patients needing artificial limbs. The student approached the Rosenbergers at Standing With Hope to become their partners.

As a result, three Belmont physical therapy students set off on a medical service trip to Ghana, led by three faculty members. They developed a new collaboration with faculty and students from the University of Accra's physical therapy program and explored the challenges physical therapists face in Ghana, which extend far beyond not having enough prosthetic devices to lack of adequate clean water, health care resources, or medical knowledge in many rural areas. The Belmont students also worked directly with amputees in supervised clinics, putting their physical therapy training to direct use and joined their Ghanan counterparts in providing exercises and training for local staff, ensuring that the best current practices would reach patients in need.

Besides the collaborative medical work with the Standing With Hope project, the Belmont team also spent time exploring the history and culture of Ghana, again collaborating with University of Accra students and faculty. This proved equally eye opening, as their hosts made clear that in Ghana material scarcity requires being able to make do in creative ways with whatever resources are available. This experience convinced the Belmont students that they needed to broaden their learning beyond the technicalities of physical therapy to understanding the larger context of their profession.

At the end of the trip, their hosts took the students to the slave castles, the prisons where enslaved Africans were kept before being sold and shipped to the Americas. As Belmont professor Renee Brown noted, this proved to be a dramatic moment for students and faculty. She found herself, as did her students, asking, "Why was I never taught this in school?" These reminders of the international dimensions of the slave trade suddenly brought the Americans' and the Ghanans' collective history into view. While the team from Belmont was learning to collaborate and serve in a professional capacity, these new connections with students at the University of Accra also brought home the ways the people from both schools were already connected across boundaries of nation and culture. Upon returning, Belmont students and faculty decided to continue and expand the project.[15]

Learning to Take Civic Action at Widener University

Andrea Stickley is a sophomore political science major at Widener University near Philadelphia, Pennsylvania. She was surprised but pleased by her meeting with former Philadelphia mayor John Street in Harrisburg, Pennsylvania. "He was glad to see college students doing something about higher education costs," she reported. Andrea was one of 50 Widener students who participated in Student Lobby Day by spending the day in the state capital and meeting with legislators to argue in favor of a pending bill called the Middle Income Debt Reduction Act. The students were joined by Widener's president, James T. Harris III, which gave a certain gravity to their meetings with state legislators and other elected officials such as Mayor Street.

"It was a fantastic experience for students," said political science professor Wes Leckrone, one of Student Lobby Day's organizers. The purpose of the trip was to educate students on how to work with elected government officials to enact real change. In this case, it was change on an issue that directly affected the students and Widener University as a whole: the problem of student debt. Many of the participating students had already spent a semester in their political science classes doing research on the issue. Some of the students were able to present their research projects to legislators as evidence in favor of the bill to reform student loan practices in Pennsylvania. "It was a fantastic experience for students," Leckrone said. "They learned more in that one day of walking around the Capitol than I could have taught them in a month of classes."

Student Lobby Day illustrates how an NAC&U institution such as Widener University can apply the strengths of its moderate size and close-knit campus community to organize educational activities, academic and extracurricular, to provide students with a powerful experience of citizenship in action. Along with the political science department, Widener's Office of Civic Engagement, which supports a variety of projects that enable students to work with and for communities in the greater Philadelphia area, and the Student Government Association orchestrated an unforgettable experience of democratic action for the whole campus community. Those who went to the state capital to lobby had already done their homework through academic research and by learning about lobbying and legislative etiquette in advance. When they returned, they took part in a number of on-campus and online events that gave them the opportunity to document and discuss what they had learned through the experience. Speaking for the Office of Civic Engagement, Elizabeth Housholder said, "Programs like this show that we really are creating democratic citizens who have the ability to structure change." Housholder hopes that Lobby Day can become an annual event.[16]

Cultivating Purpose to Foster Resilience

Belmont's service abroad and Widener's civic organizing for Student Lobby Day illustrate the meaning of the NAC&U's commitment to providing extensive opportunities for students to blend depth of professional expertise with the breadth of liberal arts learning by forging a civic purpose for their learning, which is to contribute value to their communities and the world. These experiences can prove catalytic for students, prompting a proactive stance toward their own educations. As we have seen, experiences like these can also open up unforeseen possibilities for students' learning, their careers, and their lives. And in the right campus climate, the enthusiasm these experiences generate for some students can prove infectious for others.

Growing into a mature, educated person committed to significant purposes requires living in a community where values are taken seriously and structure behavior in everyday life. A clearer understanding of this process has been emerging from research in developmental psychology. William Damon has shown the importance of forming what he calls "life purposes" for overall well-being as well as success in life.[17] By life purposes, Damon aims to distinguish particular, often shifting career goals from longer-term dispositions to "accomplish something that is at the same time meaningful to the self and consequential for the world beyond the self."[18] As an educational objective, this means enabling students to make sense of themselves, their relationships, and their context, but it also focuses attention on their connection to the larger world in its various dimensions.

For other contemporary psychologists such as Martin Seligman, the key lies in the development of a virtue he calls "grit," meaning perseverance toward goals, even in the face of obstacles and setbacks. Research makes clear that achieving such a quality activates the formation of the kind of purpose Damon describes. By orienting the individual toward significant values, purpose provides motivation to learn, pulling emerging adults out of themselves toward concern for others and the fate of the larger world.[19]

Seen in this light, a number of features of NAC&U campus life take on an added importance. Students are often struck by the availability of opportunities to continue their interests in sports and the arts, a number of which are described in later chapters. The point here, however, is that by making artistic and athletic participation available as an avocation, a university or college can help a student continue to develop skills and sensibilities that are important for personal growth and resilience and that can support further learning. In a similar way, it is noteworthy how often career counseling is connected to academic courses and experiences such as internships, study abroad, and civic engagement. These too are valuable resources for students to explore their gifts and interests in relation to possible life purposes. Campus chaplaincies and offices of religious life are also available resources. And, as we saw in the case of Widener University's Office of Civic Engagement, direct participation in shaping public debate can have powerful formative effects, helping students to grasp their own efficacy as people and citizens.

Tying Together the Three Elements of an NAC&U Education

By emphasizing the exploration of meaning and purpose, NAC&U campuses provide a variety of ways for students to connect their own need for career preparation with an understanding of the world and the needs of oneself and others. This is a powerful way to integrate students' undergraduate learning.

In their professional studies, students explore the fit between their particular interests and talents and opportunities for careers. This is how students can learn to make something of themselves in the world. As with campus life in its many dimensions—academic, social, cultural, artistic, and athletic—that help students find themselves, professional preparation is also suited to the individual needs and aims of each student.

Liberal learning is where students expand their perspectives, exploring the larger world, learning how the natural and human worlds work. Through the liberal arts they learn to think and communicate effectively under a wide horizon. They also learn to analyze, using a variety of intellectual disciplines ranging from the humanities and the arts to the social and natural sciences, and they learn how to reflect on what they discover. This large frame enables students to see how they and their aspirations relate to those of others. Here, students explore various ways of framing and analyzing experience, and they discover from many perspectives that they are parts of a larger whole that they depend on and that they share responsibility for.

This dimension of relatedness and interdependence becomes actual through engaged civic participation in which students learn to combine their particular involvement as future professionals with a larger understanding of self and the world, which they obtain from liberal learning, to realize the ideals of justice and human equality. These are the values of democratic citizenship, which the nation and the world so much needs today; they are what an NAC&U education stands for.

In turn, finding one's life purposes provides resilience in the face of adversity that enables individuals to recover direction in uncertain situations. This is clearly an especially useful capacity in a time of unstable personal prospects in a changing society. NAC&U's ongoing commitment to helping students find their life purpose is a critical contribution to American higher education.

Notes

1. Baum, Ma, & Payea, *Education Pays.*
2. Association of American Colleges and Universities, *An Introduction to LEAP.*
3. Kuh, *High-Impact Educational Practices.*
4. Chambliss & Takacs, *How College Works.*
5. Bain, *What the Best College Students Do.*
6. Staton, *A Sturdy American Hybrid.*
7. Boyer, "Creating the New American College."
8. Ayers, "The Future of Scholarship."
9. Association of American Colleges and Universities, *An Introduction to LEAP.*
10. M. Schwehn, personal communication, fall 2014.
11. G. Keller, personal communication, June 2014.
12. C. Ko & J. Both-Gragg, personal communication, December 8, 2014.
13. Manhattan College Public Affairs Office, personal communication, December 7, 2014.
14. John Carroll University, personal communication, April 16, 2015.
15. R. T. Brown, personal communication, September 8, 2014.
16. "Students Engage Legislators With Hope of Enacting Change."
17. Damon, *Path to Purpose*, p. 33.
18. Ibid.
19. Seligman, *Flourish.*

2

ONLY CONNECT

Anyone who has spent time in the American heartland can immediately recognize the signs: the sudden stillness, an eerie green spreading across a darkening sky. Tornado! "Take cover," blare the sirens. For students in the meteorology program at Valparaiso University in Indiana, however, such moments are integral to their Convective Field Study experience, 11-day courses held every May and June as the majors in the program put their academic learning and professional training to work in a real-time challenging environment.

During the field experience, which the students nicknamed "Storm Chases," the participants apply the results of their courses in the science of meteorology (e.g., atmospheric dynamics, synoptics, mesoscale meteorology, and thermodynamics) to the complex tasks of forecasting and tracking real-time severe weather on the Great Plains. The inherent technical complexity of weather forecasting in a region known for its volatile conditions presents a demanding problem in itself. "It really is where the rubber meets the road," a senior student declared. But this is a challenge the students are well prepared for. During their field experience, they augment three-dimensional analysis and forecasting of atmospheric motions with strong communication skills to effectively track the severe weather systems and warn communities in their path. There is little room for error or for miscommunication because human lives are at stake.

For 80% of Valparaiso University meteorology students who participate, this field experience serves as a pivotal link between classroom theory and real-world application. First-time participants, typically sophomores, enter this course with a solid foundation in meteorological analysis and forecasting, as well as the physical principles of atmospheric motions. Veteran participants have acquired a much deeper understanding of the linkages between theoretical principles and the severe weather conditions they encounter. Early morning weather discussions provide students with the opportunity not only to explore the atmosphere and the depth of their knowledge but also to develop liberal learning concepts, such as leadership, mentoring, and communication skills.

These field experiences allow students to learn from their professors as well as their peers in a professional environment. Upper-class students serve as mentors to first-time participants as vehicle team leaders, shepherding them through the exciting and grueling long days and cross-country miles, always cognizant of keeping each other safe in threatening weather environments. At the same time, forecasting the atmosphere is often a humbling experience where patience and perseverance are highly valued virtues; even the best forecasters occasionally sputter. Despite their rigorous training and the explosive pace of scientific advancement, students quickly learn there is still much to discover about the atmosphere.

Storm chasing exemplifies how the merger of theory and application is integrated in academic pursuit at Valparaiso University. Students come to understand how their education is much more than acquiring knowledge or a set of skills; it focuses on solving real-world problems for the betterment of society. Such experiences change the students' worldview. As a recent meteorology graduate noted, "I am extremely proud to be a Valpo alum. . . . Our faculty made sure that we developed our professional side with opportunities for research, but were also given the opportunity to be forecasters. . . . No [other school graduates] had the same repertoire as I did."[1]

What Integrated Learning Means

This chapter takes up the theme of integrated learning as a hallmark of an NAC&U education. As we saw in Chapter 1, all NAC&U institutions aim to provide their students with an education that intentionally puts together the two main areas of their academic learning: the liberal arts and professional study. Moreover, this intentional weaving of connections also aims to motivate students to engage with serving others and contributing actively to purposes beyond the individual self.

Students in courses like Valparaiso's Storm Chases are not just learning subject matter and its application to professional contexts. They are also learning how to learn. By combining the theoretical disciplines of climate science with the technical capacity to forecast and track weather events, the course blends the general competences provided by the liberal arts and sciences with the specific competences that define *meteorology* as a profession. Students were able to demonstrate their ability to put their general knowledge and specific skills to work in providing a public benefit, which embodies an integrated education.

Furthermore, according to testimonies from students and faculty, the experience changes the students. They now know that they can learn complex abilities and practice them in responsible ways. By reflecting on what they have accomplished, as the field experience challenged them to do, they discovered how to learn. Furthermore, many of them now believe that they will continue to make such learning a part of their future lives.

All this illustrates the findings of contemporary research on how learning happens and how it can be enhanced. According to modern research, effective teaching generally has four basic components, all of which are illustrated by the storm chases. First, the instructor must be explicit about what is to be learned, why it needs to be learned, and what purpose the learning serves. Second, the teacher needs to model and illustrate what is to be learned. Third, the students have to have opportunity to practice what is being learned; that is, they must be able to apply the concept or articulate the idea. And fourth, the students need feedback on their performance as well as support in surmounting difficulties.[2]

When what is to be learned is ultimately as broad and as deep and as vital for life as the integration of a wide understanding of the world with a particular way of contributing to it, which is the intent of bringing the liberal arts and professional studies together, one size rarely fits all. For this reason, the diversity among the ways NAC&U campuses approach integration is an important strength. This chapter illustrates some of that diversity of approach by going inside a number of these courses on particular campuses to show how integrated learning also encourages the learner to apply his or her learning toward serving the world.

Still, important common principles have emerged from research on learning that are useful for grasping what is going on across the range of integrative efforts at NAC&U institutions. In a study that explains the implications of today's learning theory for improving higher education research, Richard Keeling and Richard Hersh wrote,

> Learning that sticks, the kind that leads to the kind of changes we expect of college, what we call higher learning, require[s] rich engagement with new material and that the outcome of this engagement is a concrete and tangible change in the mind—a change in how one thinks and makes sense of the world.[3]

Making the critical point that studies show that colleges and universities can demonstrate quite limited success on these measures for large numbers of their students, Keeling and Hersh go on to argue that effective learning requires not only cognitive involvement on the part of learners but also important engagement of emotional energy, imagination, and perseverance.[4]

College-level learning is demonstrated by greater depth of understanding; the ability to apply new knowledge to the world; the ability to articulate and defend a new perspective; and growth in personal, social, and civic maturity. Keeling and Hersh emphasize that the available knowledge shows that "learning occurs horizontally, across experiences in and out of the classroom, vertically within majors and disciplines," and that real learning is, "necessarily, cumulative. . . . The whole is greater than the sum of the parts."[5] They argue that what is needed is "mindful, coherent, and integrated design" of curricula and learning experiences to provide appropriate challenges, demanding teaching with constructive feedback, and supportive mentoring.

The essential need, Keeling and Hersh say, is for "integrated learning." By this, they mean learning that is "personally meaningful, informs authentic problem-solving, inspires imagination, and enables further learning." Such education has to be holistic and include "identity formation as well as the development of resilience, perseverance, and emotional maturity."[6] To achieve this, student motivation is key. And this is closely related to the quality of faculty-student interaction, the sense of being engaged in a common endeavor of great value for both parties. As we will see, all these principles are at work in an NAC&U education.

Connecting the Self With the World

As Otto Raths, professor of physics at Wagner College in New York, walks in one of the two doors and down the steps to the front of the small auditorium in Spiro Hall, he pauses to look at his students. About a dozen men and women sit scattered across the room. Peering through his thick glasses, the longtime Wagner professor jabs his finger at one door or the other and asks each student, "You came in that door, right?" One after the other, they confirm his guesses. "Ha, I know how you think!" he observes. After this unusual approach to taking attendance, Raths explains to the students that this course will help them learn to think in new and better ways by, among other things, challenging the things they take for granted about the world and how it works.

This is Astronomy 108: The Solar System. However, all the students are also enrolled in its partner course, Philosophy 205: Philosophy of the Mind. Together, they make up an intermediate learning community called Exploring the Cosmos and Our Place Within It. Together, the two courses lead to bigger questions students would not be likely to study if they were taking a physics course alone, such as, What can we know about the universe and ourselves? Is it possible to know the way the universe exists and the way our minds exist? Does the universe have a purpose? Is there a place for consciousness, and for God, within a scientific view of the universe?

The purpose of this learning community is different from the first-year learning community discussed in Chapter 1, which brought together a natural science (biology) and a social science (economics) to confront the environmental problems facing a nearby community. There the students honed their thinking through the reflective tutorial from the English department. By contrast, Exploring the Cosmos and Our Place Within It targets sophomore- and junior-level students who have already completed a first-year learning community experience.

Whereas the first-year experience emphasized integrating knowledge and skill to work with local communities to solve environmental problems, this one seeks to use a natural science (astronomy) and a humanities discipline (philosophy), again supported by a reflective tutorial, to enable students to hone their ability to learn in another, equally important dimension. The two linked courses help students develop the intellectual tools to explore in sophisticated ways the meaning of today's science of the natural world for their understanding of the human place in that larger world. This knowledge poses challenges for students in deciding how to think about the implications of all this for humanity's future and how to live their own lives. One practical upshot of this experience, students report, is that they are better able to tolerate others with differing views, in part because they can understand why others hold the opinions they do.

It took a scientifically minded philosopher and a deep-thinking physicist to create a course like this. The philosopher is John Danisi, who was a double major in chemistry and philosophy during his own undergraduate years. He and Raths share a fascination with different views of the cosmos and a commitment to keep questioning and finding new answers. In Raths's lectures, therefore, he not only conveys the facts about the sun's makeup, temperature, size, and so forth but also continually contextualizes them. He tells stories (e.g., about meeting the physicist and Nobel laureate Hans Bethe), makes observations ("Absolute truth in nature is very hard to find. You never stop, but you become very humbled"), and recommends readings (like the Saturday edition of the *Wall Street Journal* and an essay by a psychologist in the *New York Times*).

While Raths deals with the makeup of the universe, Danisi is exploring what we can know about the nature of the human self from a philosophical perspective, from the ancient Hebrews and Greeks, through Descartes and Sartre, to today's scientific-materialistic thinkers, who "whittle away the mind" as a valid way of understanding the human being. "My goal is to restore a place for the mind and for God," Danisi says.

For students like sophomore Paul Passantino, who was still undecided about his major but leaning toward business, this course proved to be mind blowing and inspirational, so much so that he found that he couldn't stop talking with friends about the ideas discussed in class. "That's why I'm really loving this class," he reported.

> We can have different types of views, and I personally believe that Danisi's philosophy class has helped me with just being able to accept other people's views. Being able to learn someone else's views, and make your own opinion on it, that's the beauty of philosophy, I think. To see how things work, how people think.

After all, he pointed out, just as Galileo and Copernicus overturned the received wisdom of their day, today's students need to keep their minds open to discover the next big thing. "As students, we will take everything we learn and find new answers," he concluded. "That's our job, to better ourselves, so we can keep this country and world going, so we [aren't just] ok with the normal. We have to keep pushing the boundaries."[7]

The Virtue of Learning Communities

As we have seen in this and the preceding chapter, learning communities incorporate two or more courses, usually offered by different departments, that are linked by a common theme or problem, sometimes called "big questions." These are issues that involve the larger concerns of our time and of human life. These courses are therefore reminders of what higher education is intended to prepare its graduates to do, which is to take part in the important movements of their time. The first-year Wagner College learning community that focuses on an immediate practical question of sustainability and the more advanced learning community exemplifies this aspect of addressing important issues. Typically, each learning community requires students to read, write, and work closely with each other and with their professors. They are taught jointly by two or more faculty members, each bringing expertise in a different discipline. Students who enroll in these courses benefit from the stimulation of learning different subject matter in a common community of teachers and learners. These communities are often listed among the high-impact practices that we encountered in the previous chapter. Learning communities are clear examples of teaching practices that are intentionally designed to foster the integration of disparate viewpoints.

Some learning communities involve disciplines from the liberal arts and sciences. This is true of the two examples we have seen, one a first-year and the other an intermediate-year offering. Other forms of learning communities set out to link a professional studies course with a liberal arts offering, bringing together the general outlook of liberal learning with the preparation for specific occupations that is typical of professional studies. The purpose of that type of learning community is usually to enhance the learning of professional competence with frameworks that can provide a wide perspective on the professional work.[8]

For example, business courses that teach the skills of accounting or management can be illuminated in new ways when they are paired with psychological, historical, or sociological analyses of particular industries or countries. The result of taking part in such learning communities is frequently that students come to see how understanding human psychology or the history of particular countries can contribute to making business practices more effective while coming to understand business itself as part of a larger mosaic.

But the value of learning communities that link these disparate approaches extends beyond better understanding a particular field or specific topic. There is evidence that this kind of intentional integration, which demonstrates and teaches complex thinking that draws on several approaches but also connects them, is especially important for developing what learning theorists call "generic competences."[9] These capacities are transferable not only across intellectual fields but also across different kinds of jobs, professional fields, and many other aspects of life, including citizenship. Among these generic skills are those abilities most in demand from today's employers: knowledge of the world, the ability to think critically, personal and social responsibility, and the capacity to integrate and apply knowledge. It is noteworthy that these abilities, particularly logical, analytic, and synthetic thinking, have become the keys to well-compensated jobs and career success.[10]

There is mounting evidence that the kind of integrative thinking NAC&Us are striving to foster is particularly valuable for successful careers. For example, an influential line of research begun by Roger Martin, former dean of the Rotman School of Management at the University of Toronto, has found that certain ways of thinking set apart exceptionally successful business leaders from their less successful competitors. Martin found that while many managers attempt to apply clear but simple single-purpose approaches to business situations, the most successful leaders do something different.[11]

Martin discovered that these outstanding business leaders do not avoid complicated problems. On the contrary, they are able to keep their focus on large and complicated situations, a bit like the big questions learning communities focus on. At the same time, they are able to analyze the particular parts of the situation. According to Martin, they can trace patterns and connections among these particular aspects of the larger situation. Most important, such leaders hold conflicting possibilities together in their thinking.

This enables them to come up with what he calls "integrative solutions" to complex problems. These integrative solutions, according to Martin, are practical strategies that enable successful business leaders to successfully guide opposing forces and differing personalities toward common purposes.[12]

These, then, are corroborations from a very different sector of society of what liberal arts educators have long been arguing. One of the most important skills for success in life is the ability to think carefully in complex ways; particularly, to hold opposite and opposing ideas together in tension, to be able to place events and decisions in their appropriate contexts, and to use speaking and writing to formulate and communicate thought. Learning communities are a powerful tool at the disposal of students at NAC&U institutions who want to learn these all-important skills. The big questions posed by learning communities in the arts and sciences may be different in subject matter from the decisions faced by business leaders or other professionals (although not as different as some may think), but the challenge is the same. A good education enables students to develop similar abilities: to analyze and think critically about various sources of information, to use disparate methods of analysis, and to formulate decisions and judgments with arguments to support those judgments. These are the same challenges that will increasingly define working and living in the twenty-first century.

Capstone Courses and Projects

Among the high-impact practices endorsed by the Association of American Colleges and Universities are Capstone Courses and Projects, which are special educational experiences designed to provide students with a culminating intellectual activity that enables them to pull together and apply what they have learned.[13] As the name suggests, these projects are intended to be a kind of general taking stock of each student's most important learning in college. Not every college senior does a capstone project, but they are standard practice at NAC&U institutions.

Typically, a capstone project centers on the student's major field, perhaps taking the form of a research paper. In some majors, it may be an original work of art, a performance, or a portfolio of original work. In every case, however, the goal of the capstone project is to provide students with the chance to discover, confirm, and articulate for others the value of what they have been studying. It continues the integrative purposes of learning communities and teaches students how to reflect on their academic experience, analyzing it in ways that highlight those thinking skills so important for work and life.

Business Capstone at Ohio Northern University

Jeremiah Skow has recently graduated as a senior management and market-ing major from Ohio Northern University in Lima. Reflecting on his cap-stone experience, Jeremiah had no doubt that it required him to "apply all the skills and knowledge [he had] acquired throughout [his] college career." Besides this, he has concluded that devising a plan to identify marketing opportunities for a major multinational corporation "unlocked" his creativ-ity, and making a formal presentation to this multibillion-dollar client pro-vided a "reality shock." He said,

> I realized that, along with my teammates, while still a student I was using my knowledge to make potential decisions for a major corporation. . . . That was just what I was hoping I might be able to do after graduation.

The capstone course at Ohio Northern that roused Jeremiah's enthusi-asm is designed to enable business students to integrate their knowledge of all the business disciplines as well as their liberal arts backgrounds by chal-lenging them to develop business solutions for real clients. The class runs for two semesters and is organized in teams of four or five students, delib-erately mixing majors in management with students in accounting, finance, and marketing. The teams are assigned projects that real clients bring to the business school. In any given year, various teams may be working on a busi-ness plan for a family-owned company; devising a marketing strategy for a Fortune 500 corporation, such as Jeremiah's team did; devising green energy solutions; or addressing problems in organizing health care or manufactur-ing. The climax of the course is a series of public sessions in which each team presents its project publicly to the client. Students are assessed not only on their ability to apply business concepts to real situations but also on their level of effective teamwork, communication, and problem-solving creativity.

According to management professor Michele Govekar, the course enables seniors to move beyond their student identities into the role of business pro-fessional. "Seniors graduate knowing they can do it," commented Govekar. "They can make a real difference in the business world." Jeremiah Skow's experience illustrates how this development can happen. As he recounted his time in the course, the first task he and his teammates confronted was defining the purpose of their investigation. "The client set no boundaries and gave no direction beyond finding new marketing opportunities for their products," Jeremiah recalled. "They wanted fresh eyes on the subject."

Although exhilarating, this lack of a clear directive also aroused the team's anxiety, so organizing and managing the team of four became an important objective in itself. In the end, according to Jeremiah, the team proved to be "incredible. . . . Each member pulled his or her own weight, and they encouraged each other to work harder." But the team members, in consultation with their faculty adviser, had to figure out how to divide the tasks and get the work done on time. As a result, the students believe they acquired new or improved skills in "time management, leadership, and communication, as well as financial analysis." Their client and their professor assessed their project as very well done. As a result, all the team members graduated with what they saw as "a tremendous accomplishment" to put on their résumés, thereby earning that sense of confidence Govekar discussed. "Now," said Jeremiah, "each of us will be able to walk into a job interview knowing that being able to present evidence of this project will give you an advantage. The capstone was a game changer!"[14]

Integrating knowledge and skills through supervised professional work for an actual client does seem to have changed the nature of the game for these students. From an academic exercise it became a serious professional effort with real consequences and not just for a grade but for the client's success in the world. As a result, the students came to realize that part of professional life is the requirement that professionals take responsibility for the consequences their knowledge will have for their clients and for the larger world. The Ohio Northern business capstone teaches this extremely important lesson by allowing students to learn by doing and that using specialized business knowledge and general liberal arts skills to solve real problems also entails moral responsibility.

Capstone to an Uncommon Core Curriculum at Nazareth College

Nazareth College, near Rochester, New York, provides an interesting example of how capstone experiences work to build up students' competence in general intellectual skills while permitting students to follow their individual interests and showcase strengths. Nazareth has recently implemented a major revision of its core or required curriculum for all students, calling it an "uncommon core" to draw attention to its unusual features. The new program incorporates many new insights into how people learn. For all four undergraduate years, the new core curriculum gives students a highly interconnected set of courses and experiences known as *pathways*, which are designed to help every student get the most out of college by linking professional studies with liberal arts, including a substantial amount of experience outside the classroom that applies ideas in real situations with communities beyond the campus. The core especially tries to develop general competences of thinking that can be transferred across fields and from college to life and work.

The most noteworthy part of this new curriculum is the Core Milestone Experience, required of all students for graduation. Intended for the latter phase of the students' time at Nazareth, this course shifts the initiative in learning from the faculty to the students. It requires each student to take the initiative in designing, with faculty coaching, a capstone experience culminating in an original product that embodies the student's learning. It is not primarily a course in the student's major field but a culminating activity of the interdisciplinary core curriculum. These products are not tied to the students' major fields and may range from research papers to performances to works of invention. Their common feature, however, is that they must be built around an interest or question that has become especially important to that student during his or her undergraduate years. This is the student's "enduring question."

This question must be an integrative one, which means that it must feature "common elements, themes, and ideas that make connections across time, disciplines, and experiences." This is a broad but demanding criterion. Discerning this question and refining it to connect the various parts of the student's undergraduate career is the first important step in the capstone process. Students consult with their faculty advisers in this process, which calls into play analytical skills, imagination, and the capacity to self-evaluate and manage. These questions can cover a wide range, from the philosophical issues about what can make life worth living to issues of technological advances and environmental sustainability.

As all this suggests, a major goal of the capstone is enhancing the students' ability to evaluate their own learning, skills, and strengths as well as recognize areas of challenge where they need to apply effort to grow. Like any well-designed course, the Core Milestone Experience provides students with a clear set of learning goals in the form of the desired outcomes of the experience together with criteria for measuring them. These goals and purposes are focused on two areas. The first is the application of knowledge, including practical experience as well as academic learning, to exploring the enduring question. But the second concerns self-knowledge and the ability to reflect on one's own practice, to accept and learn from feedback on performance, and to seek to improve. In both areas, analytical rigor, creative imagination, and communication figure as essential skills.

Each student pursues an enduring question, but the course also brings advanced students together regularly in small sections with a faculty preceptor to share their learning and receive feedback on the progress of their exploration. The criteria for the evaluation of the final product of the capstone are demanding. They include a wide range of measures, including the relationship of the enduring question to various disciplines, especially the student's major; how the student's exploration of that question relates to issues and problems in today's world; and how it relates to the student's own intellectual and personal development. So the capstone incorporates elements of a learning community and forms a logical culmination of the intellectual and personal growth that the uncommon core curriculum tries to develop for all the student's years in college.

The Core Milestone Experience is intended to be a real bridge between college and life after graduation, integrating knowledge and experience from the student's whole college career. It also points toward the future, emphasizing the application of that knowledge to the larger world. Finally, it includes the students' awareness of themselves as responsible for their learning and its applications.[15]

Critical and Creative Thinking at Belmont University

The Artist's Studio is a curricular track for students of the arts in Belmont University's honors program where students are trained to integrate their professional studies as visual, performing, or literary artists with the liberal learning emphasized in their honors curriculum. The culminating activity in the program is a senior artistic project. Intended to demonstrate student mastery of critical thinking skills and the ability to apply knowledge, the project must involve some original production in the area of the student's concentration in the arts.

Dean Palya, a senior in the Artist's Studio, has taken to heart the value of blending liberal and professional learning in the execution of his project. For his capstone project he chose a full-length musical recording that tells a story of mercy and atonement and the role forgiveness plays in human experience, classic themes of some of the world's greatest literature. Dean employed his study of literature to give added direction and depth to his creative musical endeavor.

Following a yearlong study of the structure of narrative with a playwright and a professor of literary theory, as the first phase of his senior capstone, Dean developed a story treatment about a police detective forced by tragedy to discover the importance of grace and forgiveness. After allowing an innocent man to be convicted, the detective falls into a deep depression, befriends a stranger with a dark past of his own, and eventually discovers a secret that forces them both to make a crucial choice about their futures.

To tell this story, Dean composed, recorded, and produced a musical work incorporating musical motifs, including distinctive instrumentation for the several characters as devices for the music to unfold the narrative. This complicated and time-consuming process required soliciting feedback and rewriting in the light of this feedback. He first composed an instrumental condensed score and then wrote lyrics prompted by the score and the prose of the story itself. Once he had a narrative score with lyrics, he went on to orchestrate the piece, which required arranging and notating the music until he finally felt ready to produce and record the completed score in his home studio. Dean was able to draw on his previous training as a musician and an audio engineer. This allowed him to perform or program all the parts himself, using a full palette of instrumentation. He mixed the individual tracks into the work so that it would play as a single connected piece (much like Gershwin's *Rhapsody in Blue*) and mastered the final product into a polished, professional recording.

While he was creating the score and developing the complete piece, Dean was also writing program notes that demonstrated his breadth of knowledge in the literary and dramatic repertoire that dealt with similar themes. He was able to employ a spectrum of influences from literature, film, and music, ranging from Dostoyevsky's *Crime and Punishment* and Langston Hughes's *Everyman's Library Pocket Poets* to Steven Spielberg's *Schindler's List* to Robert Glasper's *Black Radio* and Vince Guaraldi's *Essential Standards*. Besides using the work of such celebrated narrative theorists as Robert McKee and Syd Field, he drew deliberately on composers such as John Williams and Hans Zimmer.[16]

Integrating Learning at Pacific Lutheran University

These examples from Ohio Northern University, Nazareth College, and Belmont University show that capstones can range from producing research for actual clients, to integrating several disciplines to address a significant issue or problem, to producing creative works that incorporate analytical and compositional skills into artistic performance. These examples provide a sense of why capstones are often cited as educational experiences that make significant impacts on the students who undertake them. They have yet wider effects on the clients and audiences, including the classes and campuses where the works are presented.

Pacific Lutheran University (PLU) in Tacoma, Washington, provides yet another variation on the capstone theme. One salient aspect of PLU's use of capstones, which are required of all seniors regardless of major, is that they emphasize an individualized approach to integrating knowledge that draws on the university's strong student-faculty relationships. Jan Lewis, associate provost for curriculum at PLU, points out that the capstone courses are deliberately crafted to enable students to integrate learning from perspectives that they have been pursuing in their major field and by working with faculty members they have known through that process. "Capstones at PLU can serve multiple purposes," she said. "They vary widely depending on the discipline." For example, Lewis notes that "for education majors, a capstone involves a synopsis of the student learning experience and how that impacted the classroom experience," while "for arts majors, it may mean crafting a performance or a musical number."

As at many NAC&U institutions, students at PLU have the option of choosing among a wide range of formats for their capstone project, including scientific experiment or study, case studies related to a discipline, or writing a report on internship or field-based practicum or a thesis or research paper. The point, however, is the same: Students must exhibit their capacity to synthesize what they have learned in ways that "demonstrate capacity in specific professional standards."

The PLU capstones challenge students to demonstrate mastery of a field. For students majoring in professional studies, such as education majors, this means combining theoretical knowledge from their courses in their major with practical experience in supervised practice to achieve an understanding of the profession they aspire to join after graduation. For interdisciplinary majors, the capstone project is likely to be a venue for considering issues and problems from multiple theoretical lenses and points of view. The aim is to learn how to apply knowledge in the service of illuminating or solving real and complex problems in the sciences and technology, in society, or in culture and the arts.

Whatever the subject and whatever its format, the capstone project is always set up to push students' boundaries. Students work in a community context that is intended to push and challenge them, but they also always work with a faculty member, or sometimes several faculty members, who knows the student and the student's earlier work. PLU's capstones combine the challenge of new learning, which we have seen is essential for intellectual growth, with strong support for exploring a new area or an enduring area of interest in a new, more synthetic way.

Jan Lewis says that enabling students to be able to give good answers to the question, "What did you really learn in college?" as a way to demonstrate how they have grown in intellectual scope and maturity is a key objective of the senior capstone requirement. "It is very easy to get into a check list mode and to think that by checking off requirements you just automatically learned something," she adds. "But a capstone forces you to ask: 'What have I really learned? How did it affect me? How did it—or will it—affect the world?'"[17]

Integrated Thinking as a Way of Life: Experiential Learning

The discoveries of modern learning science have reinforced the venerable notion that we can learn in lasting ways and often grasp the significance of ideas best when we can observe the effects of ideas in our own experience.[18] That is, concepts have special impact when their significance becomes manifested in experience. Philosophers have argued that all serious learning is a kind of learning by doing. We do not simply absorb knowledge. We have to assimilate new impressions and ideas; to make them our own, we have to learn how to use them to expand our understanding.

The learning sciences have extended this insight by careful study of how experts function in various areas of activity, from scientists to chess masters to musicians to athletes. Despite all the differences in their specific areas of knowledge, experts in every domain share two traits: They have good recall of knowledge they have organized well through practice, and they can quickly and effectively spot significant patterns and use them to guide their application of knowledge to situations.[19] Because they lack precisely these two abilities, beginners in every domain must set about a laborious process of developing expertise by starting with explicit rules and procedures for thinking and only gradually approach the abilities shared by experts.

The clear implication of research into learning by figures such as John Seely Brown, Allan Collins, Susan Newman, Paul Duguid, and others is that faculty-student interaction associated with effective learning involves some form of cognitive apprenticeship leading to intellectual development.[20] Such an "apprenticeship of the mind" allows the learner to enter the world of the expert in carefully staged and monitored steps. Such learning is essentially a learning in context, in that what is being learned is understood in ways that connect with the practice the learner is apprenticed to.

This rich body of research sheds light on the often subtle dynamics of teaching and learning. We have already noted the four fundamental concepts identified as characteristic of well-designed educational experiences. Teaching requires being clear and explicit in articulating the goals and purposes of what is to be learned; modeling the practices to be learned; and providing feedback that guides learners toward a more competent imitation of expertise, and support, or what is called *scaffolding*, which makes it easier for students to imitate the teacher's performance. As students grow in competence with the practice, especially as they begin to approach real expertise, the explicit rules and guides can then be gradually withdrawn by the teacher.[21]

In effect, these principles suggest that robust learning of complex intellectual practices requires learning by doing. It requires practice, feedback on that practice, learner response to the feedback, and recurrent attention to the goals and procedures that make up the field. In that sense all learning for mastery of a discipline or skill is experiential learning. But because expertise is something shared among members of a community who have mastered certain practices, the cycle of modeling, imitation, feedback, and improvement typically takes place within such communities. In its most basic sense, then, all pedagogy is a community's organized practice for shaping expertise in aspiring new members.

Still, it is easy to overlook the fact that any practice that requires intense concentration necessarily shapes the learner's attitudes. The stronger and more effective, or the higher the impact of, the pedagogy, the more formative it is likely to be of the student's disposition, not only toward the subject matter but also toward learning itself. Seen in this perspective, a characteristic of NAC&U's emphasis upon integrated learning is its effort to cultivate a sense of personal investment in the value of learning and a sense of purpose regarding the use of knowledge. For promoting these goals, connection and community turn out to be fundamental.

Cultivating an Integrative Stance at the University of La Verne

For years students at the University of La Verne in Southern California have worked toward their senior capstone as a culminating experience of their four years. For their part, university administrators have hoped that by making the capstone a primary focus during the junior and senior years, students would develop a greater understanding and clarity about their focus after graduation. La Verne conducted a study of the effectiveness of its integrated core curriculum, which includes the capstone. As a result, administrators have further refined their approach, preparing students earlier than ever to begin thinking actively about their areas of study and the people they hope to be.

All students at La Verne participate in the La Verne Experience, an integrative model of education that weaves theory and practice through a variety of curricular and cocurricular experiences. Building on the university's values, the aim of the La Verne Experience is to broaden students' knowledge regardless of their major, program, or level of study. To this end, the institution has been bringing reflective practices into the whole range of students' educational experiences.

For students like Hayley Hulin, starting the thinking process sooner rather than later is welcome. A sophomore honors student, Hayley had participated as a freshman in a FLEX (First-Year La Verne Experience) learning community. She joined 18 of her peers in three bundled courses plus a writing course to help the students tie together two different disciplines and reflect on their learning. For example, the Good Life FLEX course is taught by two full-time professors, one from economics and the other from philosophy, to connect the students in a practical, hands-on way with community agencies that serve groups struggling with achieving a good life for themselves and their families. Concern for the larger society, Hayley and her peers have been learning, is an integral value for the university community.

Even prior to her first day of classes, Hayley was embraced by the campus and its values and was able to reflect on her own. "I participated in Community Engagement Day with nearly 600 of my peers and La Verne faculty," she said, and described her experience volunteering at a domestic abuse shelter for women and children in Los Angeles. "I helped paint houses for these families and spent time gardening. I really appreciated watching our professors, my professors, who spent the day working alongside us." Emphasizing how important this experience has been for her, Hayley said,

> For the first time, I was able to talk to my professors in advance of starting the semester. We had the chance to be human together, working toward the same thing, and that enhanced my respect and admiration for them even before I experienced them in the classroom.

Other students have had similar responses to the La Verne Experience and its emphasis on connecting learning with service to the society. The aim of the FLEX program, as well as its sophomore successor, SoLVE (Sophomore La Verne Experience) is to enable students to "gain context" to cultivate a particular approach toward their learning, their world, and themselves. Adam Plax, a sophomore business major, described his experience as "definitely a life-changer for me. . . . It has opened me up to try new things and become involved in many different things on campus . . . and become more socially active and business-minded."

La Verne's core values are based in a disposition that could be characterized as thoughtful and engaged. The idea of stance, or fundamental disposition, how you see the world around you and how you see yourself in that world, is what Roger Martin, business theorist, believes underlies all particular attitudes.[22] Martin's studies of successful business leaders revealed that they were set apart by sharing a stance he called "integrative." An integrative stance, according to Martin, leads people to constantly strive to develop greater understanding of the world they inhabit, while also working to improve their expertise and the quality of the communities in which they find themselves.[23]

To promote cultivation of an integrative stance, La Verne has been encouraging practices of reflection throughout the student's whole curriculum. As part of their freshman year, students reflect through an essay examining their feelings about the linked classes of their freshman learning community. This process continues the following year in SoLVE and culminates in a final autobiography as part of the senior capstone. Through this learning practice, students are also challenged to look within themselves to ask how efforts inside and outside the classroom tie to the bigger picture of their hopes and lives. Following each community engagement experience, and each part of the core curriculum, students are requested to ask themselves such questions as, What is it? Why do we do it? Is it important? By repeating these questions, students are forming habits of mind that will serve them well, not only in their college careers but also in their lives after graduation. Students are learning to cultivate an integrated stance toward their experience.[24]

Integrating by Design at Drury University

Because professional studies prepare students in knowledge and skills that directly affect other people and the larger world, they are well suited for learning that is engaging, personal, and responsive to purposes beyond the self. These features are well illustrated in teaching design, a practice that unites several disciplines ranging from engineering to computer science to architecture. Designing requires a considerable personal investment of time and energy and draws on a variety of skills and areas of knowledge. Especially in architecture, which spans the fine arts and the engineering sciences, the design process entails not only analytical acumen but also creative imagination. Like visual artists, architects must be imaginative yet use their imagination to solve problems in the actual world. Additionally, because their products have an immediate and large impact on society, they must also learn to work with clients and communities to achieve solutions that others will be willing to live not only with but also in.

A project by students at the Hammons School of Architecture at Drury University in Springfield, Missouri, was the main activity in an advanced architectural design class titled Landscapes of Resilience: Butterfly Garden and Overlook Design and Construction. The project was funded by the Tariq Khamisa Foundation, which was also supporting a parallel design project in New York City to help communities recover following the devastation from Hurricane Sandy. For the Drury students, a tornado that ripped through nearby Joplin destroyed houses, families, and lives, wounding the closely knit town. The Drury students were given a direct and significant problem to solve using their architectural training: Design a physical memorial garden that would help the residents of Joplin mourn their loss and recover confidence for the future. Three residential lots in the neighborhood that had been devastated by the tornado had been set aside for the memorial. The Cunningham family home was on one of the lots, situated on a small rise that overlooked the rest of the former neighborhood. The project extended over three years and included a research fund to study how open spaces such as gardens and memorials could help communities and individuals remember and recover, and so promote resilience.

To design the project, Drury faculty worked with government agencies and professional architectural firms in Joplin and in New York. Nancy Chikaraishi of the School of Architecture directed the students' design work, while Peter Meidlinger of the English department taught a humanities class, The Healing of Joplin, to collect and edit stories of the disaster from residents of Joplin. These stories were read and analyzed by the architecture students to enable them to better imagine the nature of what was to be remembered and healed by their design. The stories helped the students understand the people this project connected them with and helped them listen more sensitively to the members of the community.

The goals and learning outcomes of the course were multiple and demanding, so the course was thereby providing a good experience of what actual architectural practice is like. The problem to be solved required students to "create one, unified, healing garden space." The first goal required the students to research what was known about the relationship between garden design and medical and psychological healing and then apply that knowledge to the actual design process. The solution also had to include four elements: "a portal, a path, a destination, and a sense of surround." All this had to fit within the three residential lots, a parcel of land that focused on the former Cunningham house. The second goal was to develop design skills by meeting these criteria, and the third goal was to create actual construction documents so the idea could be translated in actual layout and structure.

In addition to these goals, which included knowledge of the context, informed by the students' training in the liberal arts and reinforced by the Healing of Joplin humanities class, and the professional skills of design and construction, the course also specified a series of personal capacities essential to successful architectural practice. Students were to be assessed on their levels of competence in "leadership and communication skill" as well as their ability to work with classmates on teams responsible for various features and stages of the design. But beyond this, the course syllabus listed three kinds of experience students were expected to acquire: "construction experience as an architect in an office . . . giving back to [one's] community . . . [and] understanding that there are things that are greater than ourselves."

Throughout the semester, the students were placed in teams that imitated the actual organization of an architectural office. They had deadlines to meet, they held sessions in which proposals and models were presented and criticized, and they had to agree on final specifications, all while working with actual contractors and suppliers in the field.

The final design melded the students' research and liberal arts understanding of issues of grieving and remembering with their growing expertise in design and construction. The portal to the site was designed to mark it off as sacred to the memory of those who had died there, standing where the front door of the Cunningham house had once been. Black steel tube frames outlined the house and the two adjacent to it. Beyond this stark portal, a winding, labyrinth-like path through the garden provided visitors with a protected area to remember loved ones or the community's tragedy. The design included four separate spaces, each containing a bench, a waterproof journal, and a small water feature to suggest tranquility and renewal. The park has become a destination for many visitors seeking to reconnect with the community that was shattered by the tornado. A "Butterfly Trail" through what is now known as Cunningham Park will eventually connect the new gardens to an existing park.[25]

Conclusion: "Learning That Sticks"

Richard Keeling and Richard Hersh's summary of the import of today's learning research was noted earlier in this chapter: "Learning that sticks, the kind that leads to the kind of changes we expect of college, what we call higher learning, require[s] rich engagement with new material."[26] Prompted by teaching and a climate that stimulates significant challenge and support, learning also depends on a deep engagement of emotional energy, imagination, and perseverance. This learning is manifested in the ability to apply new knowledge to the world; articulate and defend a new perspective; and grow in personal, social, and civic maturity areas.[27] They called the outcome of this kind of demanding process *integrated learning*. Keeling and Hersh concluded that this is the most valuable outcome of a college education and so ought to be seen as its measure and goal. Too often in higher education as a whole, they lamented, it is not.[28]

The samples of different kinds of connected learning presented in this chapter illustrate the principles of truly transformative higher learning. These particular cases are drawn from a wider number of possible examples of integrated learning at NAC&U institutions, but there is a strong connecting thread. Each course, learning community, or capstone project embodies a particular institution's deliberate and serious effort to make the integration among liberal arts, professional studies, and civic learning effective. Each of these experiences is also a part of a curriculum each institution is working to improve. However, these courses, and the curricula they provide windows into, are parts of the larger life of an NAC&U campus that creates and sustains the climate where integrated learning can take place and students can develop their potential as individuals and as members of a community. Chapter 3 explores how the NAC&U experience of campus life interweaves learning with personal and social growth.

Notes

1. M. Schwehn, personal communication, April 2014.

2. These ideas have become widely disseminated. For a seminal statement, see Bransford, Brown, & Cocking, *How People Learn*, pp. 133–155.

3. Keeling & Hersh, *We're Losing Our Minds*, p. 7.

4. Ibid.

5. Ibid., p. 21.

6. Ibid., p. 133.

7. Barlament, "Exploring the Cosmos."

8. Kuh, *High-Impact Educational Practices*.

9. Richard Arum and Josipa Roksa analyze and discuss the literature on defining and measuring generic intellectual competences in *Aspiring Adults Adrift*, pp. 18–21.

10. Arum & Roksa, *Aspiring Adults Adrift*, pp. 18–21.

11. Martin, *The Opposable Mind*.

12. Ibid., pp. 111–115.

13. Kuh, *High-Impact Educational Practices*, p. 11.

14. Dicke College of Business, personal communication, December 14, 2014.

15. Ohio Northern University, personal communication, December 14, 2014.

16. Belmont University, personal communication, December 19, 2014.

17. Personal communication, December 19, 2014.

18. Bransford et al., *How People Learn*, pp. 133–155.

19. Brown, Collins, & Duguid, "Situated Cognition and the Culture of Learning."

20. Collins, Brown, & Newman, "Cognitive Apprenticeship"; Brown et al., "Situated Cognition and the Culture of Learning."

21. Collins et al., "Cognitive Apprenticeship."

22. Martin, *The Opposable Mind*, pp. 111–115.

23. Ibid.

24. P. Rodman, personal community, December 19, 2014.

25. N. Chikaraishi, personal communication, December 18, 2014.

26. Keeling & Hersh, *We're Losing Our Minds*, p. 7.

27. Ibid., p. 21.

28. Ibid.

3

FINDING YOURSELF

Hayley Hulin, the sophomore at the University of La Verne in Southern California from Chapter 2, described the kind of community she experienced at her campus before classes began and throughout her university career (see p. 46). The weekend before her freshman semester, she joined 600 other freshmen and faculty members in community engagement activities, which allowed her to meet fellow incoming freshman and faculty, engage in community-based activities, and understand the mission of the university. Besides welcoming and helping guide the incoming students, this experience deepened Hayley's own connections with the campus community, especially the faculty. She said that the opportunity to interact with her professors before the semester began enhanced her respect and admiration for them.

As a sophomore, Haley continued the La Verne Experience by taking part in the Sophomore La Verne Experience (SoLVE) program. SoLVE builds on the strength of the first-year FLEX program to increase the likelihood of student success inside and outside the classroom. The continuing, integrated quality of these programs is important in enabling students to engage effectively with all the dimensions of what can otherwise appear to be a bewildering plethora of demands and choices. This chapter highlights a number of efforts at NAC&U campuses that make important contributions toward students' ability to mature and develop as whole people while they expand their range of knowledge and skills.

Welcoming Students to Belmont University

At Belmont University in Nashville, Tennessee, students are introduced to the expectations of the college experience even before they arrive on campus. Each incoming student receives preorientation homework, in the form of an online series of learning modules with interactive videos and short quizzes, while parents are encouraged to read the same material on an open-access website. The theme of the homework is how to approach and become involved in a liberal arts education, along with useful explanations on how to navigate online registration for courses.

When students and their parents arrive on campus at the opening of the fall semester, they are not left on their own. In the second stage of new student orientation, large-group sessions called Foundations are held for parents and students followed by small-group academic advising meetings. The goal is to answer questions and make sure all new students understand the procedures and the opportunities available to them. The primary theme is for students to take ownership and responsibility for their own educational progress. This theme is carried further in Welcome Week, when the focus shifts to the value of involvement in cocurricular life that complements but extends beyond classroom learning. In a number of settings, students are introduced to empirical evidence that shows how campus involvement aids learning and personal maturity while also learning the details of Belmont's expectations in their behavior and contributions to campus life.

Throughout the Belmont orientation process, as at the University of La Verne and many other NAC&U institutions, student volunteers are crucial to its success. New students and their parents meet many of these volunteers and through these encounters gain an inside perspective on the community they are about to join. Faculty members volunteer in large numbers as well, often providing that personal connection with academic life that students such as Hayley Hulin find so valuable. Through the orientation process, incoming students also have opportunities for personal conversations with a number of student services personnel whom they will need to interact with later in their campus careers. For all students, the first encounters with campus, new peers, future teachers, and counselors are exciting times. They often prove to be influential times as well because there is no other moment when students are likely to be more enthusiastic and open to the college experience than during their first weeks as new students.

The experiences of these students are good but hardly unusual examples of what it is like to live and learn at their institutions. One of the consistent comments made by graduates of NAC&Us is that along with opportunities to learn and find a career path, they most appreciate the quality of community life on their campus. NAC&U campus administrators are intentional about integrating their students, who are from varying backgrounds and locales, into their campus communities. In this new setting, orientation programs demonstrate that the new students will be able to discover new worlds of knowledge; find professors who care deeply about their fields and their students; meet new friends; and continue or start to cultivate interest in music, sports, and the arts, drama, publications, and clubs—in short, become members of a vibrant community in which they can take pride. To reap these benefits, however, students also need to be active participants and take responsibility for their participation in campus life.[1]

From Student Life to Alumni Collaboration at St. Edward's University

One measure of the power of campus community can be found in how it leads to continuing involvement on the part of graduates. As discussed in Chapter 1, the mentor program at Manhattan College gives alumni the chance to provide guidance to students who are exploring possible careers, thereby weaving connections among current students and the alumni community. At St. Edward's University in Austin, Texas, the early orientation of new students is complemented by a program for senior student leaders. Each year, the student life office and the alumni office invite 25 student leaders to become part of a monthly discussion meeting with the university's top administrators. At meetings of the Hilltop Leaders, the students have the opportunity to meet and talk with a variety of guest speakers from outside the campus, several of whom are always graduates of St. Edward's.

These discussions allow seniors to observe the campus's academic leaders in conversation with leaders from other sectors of society and to interact with them on issues of common interest, often moving into topics involving current campus events, individual administrators' educational philosophy, and students' reflection on their four years on campus. While part of the intent of this series of colloquies is to encourage students' future involvement in alumni activity, it is also conceived as part of the educational process, a chance for students in their final year at the institution to reflect on how their experiences have begun to shape their trajectories beyond graduation. Some students explicitly relate these discussions to their earlier involvement as volunteers in freshman orientation. "I did things then I usually wouldn't push myself to do," said one senior.

> I was put in situations that I wasn't comfortable with and where I made mistakes. But I slowly learned my lessons [from volunteering to work with newer students] so that through the years I have come to understand the interlinking of academics, social justice, and networking.

Summarizing a similar trajectory, another student declared he was "more confident and not willing to give up no matter how many challenges and failures [he faces]."

Other participants in the group singled it out as one of the highlights of their college career because it has prompted an exchange of stories about their undergraduate years in ways that have enabled the students to see how their involvement in campus life has helped them to expand their understanding of their potential. "It opened my eyes to the possibilities of growth and success out there," noted one participant. Other students reported a greater sense of what the mission of St. Edward's, a Roman Catholic institution, really means. In another student's words:

> The mission seems to me to be about finding yourself within the scope of learning about diversity and the whole, that everyone is different and has their own strengths . . . [and] learning about myself as a person through learning more about others and about the world.

Or, as another participant, who "came from a small town where everyone was the same religion, race, and socioeconomic level," put it: "St. Edward's opened my eyes to how diverse the world really is and made me take a hard look at how inclusive I was in my own life." Yet another student felt the campus as affirming her Catholic identity but differently than in high school: "Here it's authentic, not a buzzword or a plug. . . . It's a place of true acceptance, encouragement, and support." This student also said she thought Pope Francis would be enthusiastic about the institution.

A significant part of the stories these Hilltop Leaders tell the institution's administrators and each other centers on how their various involvements and relationships on campus contributed to an enhanced sense of self-knowledge and confidence. They emphasized especially the interest shown in their learning by some of their professors, membership in campus teams and organizations, support for cultivating a spiritual life, and forming what they believe will be long-term friendships. "I've been able to stay involved in community service," observed one student. "I've been involved as a student leader and really learned a lot across and not only within a single academic discipline."

These effects can be long lasting and grow over time. Matthew Abbot, class of 2003, heads a college prep charter school for disadvantaged youth in Austin. He is a regular participant in new student orientation at St. Edward's, as well as serving on the career services roundtable. He credits his time at the university with nurturing the principle he tries to use to guide his decisions— "to make the world a little better"—as well as the self-confidence to act on this principle. Another graduate, Victoria Gutierrez Pineda, class of 2004, is an assistant vice chancellor at Texas Tech Health Sciences Center, where she continues a career in nonprofit fund-raising. She too remains active in alumni affairs, advocating for students who now attend St. Edward's. Victoria has also been very involved in alumni affairs, establishing a scholarship in memory of her father and in honor of her mother. She sums up her reasons for continuing to be involved in the life of the university when she says, "St. Edward's helped to shape my values because of the people it brought into my life."[2]

The Social Ecology of Learning: The Educational Value of Community

The findings of much research over the past several decades underscore Victoria Pineda's testimony. Success in college and its positive effects on graduates' lives are very much the result of the people colleges bring together and the quality of the relationships they sustain. Research makes it clear that participation in orientation activities by new students, whether they are starting their first year or transferring from other institutions, makes it easier for students to integrate into the campus community.[3] Participation in orientation also makes it significantly less likely that students will withdraw from college. And once students are integrated into their campus community in positive and satisfying ways, they continue to value and celebrate the college experience. Living in an environment in which they feel they belong fosters persistence. The findings in this regard have remained strongly positive over several decades.[4]

Stories like the ones we have heard are indirect indicators of the strength of campus community sought by NAC&U institutions through programs such as freshman orientation and senior groups like the Hilltop Leaders. The power and educational value of a strong and healthy campus community enable individuals to grow and flourish, to find themselves. In the process, as the examples of continuing alumni involvement illustrate, these individuals have discovered that they become more truly who they are by thinking beyond themselves. That is, they become uniquely themselves by making connections with others and contributing to the larger life of their communities for those who follow them in the community but also, as we shall see later in this chapter, in the larger world as well.

One of the most cited problems in undergraduate education is widespread student disengagement from academics. Recent studies have analyzed this phenomenon and proposed various explanations for its worrying persistence.[5] However, it is also clear that far from being a fixed trait, student motivation is dynamic and malleable. Here the research is hopeful and helpful in pointing out the factors that are most effective in prompting students toward deeper engagement with their learning in college. The two major

factors that enable students to connect to the college enterprise are the quality of social relationships and students' development of a sense of purpose
that makes learning meaningful.[6] Student engagement with learning can be
significantly increased when students come to feel they belong, when they
discover a social and an intellectual home.[7] Likewise, discovering purpose in
life strongly motivates academic achievement. Moreover, these two factors,
social connection and purpose, are mutually reinforcing and almost always
found together.[8]

According to sociologists Daniel F. Chambliss and Christopher G.
Takacs, "College works when it provides a thick environment of constant
feedback, driven by the establishment and maintenance of social relationships."[9] Institutions of higher education are not facilities for producing a
product called the graduate. Rather, they are communities in which the out-
put of student learning cannot be separated from the participants' involvement with the purposes and relationships that define the community. The
means, in other words, are integral to achieving the ends of the enterprise.
In that sense, educational institutions function organically. Or as Chambliss and Takacs emphasize, "Learning fundamental skills is not simply about
picking up little boxes of techniques and rules. . . . It's about relating, and
wanting to relate, to this teacher, these peers, this college." In regard to learning, they insist, "the real issue is *motivation*, which is heightened by knowing
that an audience—really a person—cares."[10]

As Chambliss and Takacs expand on the insight they drew from their
10-year study of student life at a selective liberal arts college:

> Writing is really about clarifying one's ideas for others, asserting one's con-
> clusion, and respecting one's audience. . . . Critical thinking is less about
> the details of data analysis and more about the willingness—even the cour-
> age—to challenge others' arguments. And just as clearly, when students
> don't care about relating to others in these ways, learning stops.[11]

That is why the interest professors show in students' learning can have profound educative effects. It is also why becoming a part of the campus community is so crucial for academic success. College success is ultimately about
"a concerted effort to 'join the group' in the face of overwhelming, constant
feedback from other people."[12] That means, of course, that the institution
must be well organized to foster these efforts at joining the learning community and be effective at providing the feedback students need to keep their
engagement and grow in positive directions.

Attention to the quality of campus community—cultivating the social
ecology of learning in a particular place among particular people—is, then,

another key element of the model of improved undergraduate education we are seeking. Along with courses of study that integrate the broad aims of the liberal arts with the development of professional competence and a sense of civic responsibility, and the extensive use of practices of teaching and learning that engage and promote student learning through employment of high-impact practices tested by research, effective college education requires a campus community climate characterized by inclusive yet demanding expectations shared by students and faculty that support healthy relationships and personal growth.

Coming Together and Reaching Out

How do belonging and purposeful interaction with faculty and peers produce these positive effects? Answering this question requires us to understand the social processes that underlie the experience of campus community. In turn, grasping these underlying social processes makes it possible to understand why certain features of campus life are so important for student development. Understanding these underlying processes can help strengthen the factors that stimulate and support intellectual development as well as personal growth.

Some campuses have strikingly positive effects on the students who study there. Research has shown that these students thrive because of the effects of a superior campus climate. These effects are traceable not only to curricula but also to extracurricular programs that reinforce the institution's mission and the key values of its academic program. These extracurricular activities are sometimes entirely student led. In other instances, they are guided by faculty or student life staff who document and regularly take stock of program effectiveness in promoting the values espoused by the institution.[13] Participation in such activities and organizations, which can range from amateur athletics and musical performances to clubs and service organizations, builds morale, motivates engagement, and links individual students from disparate backgrounds with one another.[14]

Call4Backup at Nazareth College

At Nazareth College in Rochester, New York, Daniela Albano recalls discovering in her freshman year the campus's all-female, a cappella group, Call4Backup. Daniela noted that the audition in that first fall in college was not the kind of stress-inducing, competitive ordeal sometimes portrayed in TV shows like *Glee* or *American Idol*. "What I loved about the audition was that the members of the group first sang for *us*. It was a great way to hear what they sounded like and got me excited about auditioning." Daniela was joining a group that debuted in 1998, which antedated the current vogue of a cappella groups. Call4Backup is made up of 15 students and is completely run by its members, with no faculty or staff involvement. This means that the group chooses and arranges its own songs, runs rehearsals, and books its own singing gigs, which amount to 12 to 15 performances in any given semester.

"When we decide who is going to be in the group, we really look at personality and how well that person will mesh with the rest of us," reported Jessica Stevens, a coleader of Call4Backup. "We're not necessarily looking for the next pop star." What they are looking for, along with vocal ability, are singers who share the group's interest in using their vocal gifts to provide community service. "We've performed for free at events like Take Back the Night and the national Interfaith Understanding Conference. It's important for us to give back and volunteer whenever we can." Daniela noted that despite its independence, Nazareth College is very proud of the group and so are most students: "Whenever we perform, we definitely feel the love from the students." As an example of the group's impact, the International Championship of Collegiate A Cappella took place at Nazareth in 2012.

Call4BackUp's Impacts on Participants

For some members of the group, singing together has brought connections that have led them to continue singing after graduation and even to make it an ongoing part of their lives. Recent graduate Katelyn Marasco found that being part of the group was a highlight of her undergraduate years. "It gave me the opportunity to meet people on other campuses and especially in the music field that I otherwise would not have known," Katelyn said. "It has also led to a few job opportunities for me as well." Katelyn continues to sing in what she describes as a local, semiprofessional group called Cut Off. In addition, she noted,

> I have had the opportunity to teach at a cappella festivals, lead a masterclass in a cappella singing at other institutions, and record a CD. . . . I would not have even known that I enjoyed a cappella music if I hadn't been a part of Call4Backup. It has definitely helped shape who I am now.

Underlying Call4Backup's activity is the social process of coming together or bonding, which is common in the creation of many kinds of groups, but it can have especially powerful effects on college campuses. A number of social investigators have converged in defining four characteristics of this process, all of which are visible in Call4Backup. First, coming together is about mutual engagement, typically face-to-face, that is frequent and sustained over time. Second, the individuals involved are focused on the same object of attention, which is their musical performance. Third, they are enabled to keep this joint focus of attention because they have evolved some shared practices or patterned activities with a ritualized, repeated form, such as rehearsals, performances, and annual auditions. Fourth, these activities set up clear boundaries between those who share the activity and those who do not, helping to maintain the intensity of the group's focus. Although ritualized, these practices are far from mere empty rituals. On the contrary, they are ongoing sources of collective energy. Through continued meeting, enacting the same patterns of relating to the same objects of common attention, coming together enables individuals to trust each other enough to cooperate for mutual benefit. Thus, a virtuous cycle can be built: The willingness to trust others and share the tasks of the group is rewarded by the benefits of mutual aid and the pleasures of fellowship.[15]

Call4Backup's coming together builds up ties that last, even beyond graduation. Moreover, participation in the group can cultivate new purposes in its members, such as incorporating musical performance into their future lives, as Katelyn Marasco described. It is interesting in this connection that historian William McNeill, who is one of the thinkers responsible for identifying the underlying social process at work here, claims that the inspiration for his work came from reflecting on his own experience as a young man with the military drill: Keeping together in time, participating in shared rhythmic activity, and giving voice to the experience, McNeill discovered, created strong feelings of common purpose and belonging that became powerful motivators for the recruits, such as himself, who took part in them.[16]

The results of bonding processes are therefore noteworthy. They enable campus organizations of all kinds, including degree programs and academic honors programs, to provide a sense of being at home that is crucial to student motivation and commitment to academic work. They establish networks of mutual respect that are very valuable, particularly for students new to the college experience. Coming together provides individuals with trusted allies they can turn to for perseverance in the face of challenges. As Chambliss and Takacs discovered in their study of campus life, the resulting "microcommunities" provide the networks for most students to find friends, which is reported by alumni as the most valuable single result of their undergraduate years.[17] These networks of trust set mutual respect as the common expectation of how others should be treated. This shared expectation of respect in turn supports the willingness to trust others. The threat of being cut off from sharing in the network of trust and respect for violations of loyalty and trust is a serious deterrent to defection. Coming together is therefore a social process that fosters personal virtue as well as the resilience of group ties.

However, the very intensity that such bonding practices foster, although the engine of energy and motivation and the source of trust that makes sharing and cooperation in groups possible, builds up a strong sense of exclusivity. The result can be élan within the group but competitiveness toward other groups or even hostility toward outsiders. The danger is narrowness of purpose and restriction of empathy. (Think of sports rivalries between universities, e.g., an affect that can quickly become corrosive when directed toward other campus groups.) Strong bonding, however useful for campus culture, is clearly not enough to ensure that undergraduate life achieves its educational aims, particularly the American collegiate purpose of cultivating civic responsibility and the cooperative virtues of citizenship.

Cultivating a Proactive Stance: Civic Culture on Campus

Educational aims require a second social process, one that moves on an opposing but complementary vector to coming together: reaching out. We have already seen it in action among the a cappella singers at Nazareth College. Jessica Stevens said it was important for members of the group to support not only a dedication to their music but also an ethic of service, using their singing to give back to college and community. Just as cities, regions, and nations, campuses and schools have social climates. On some campuses, reaching out seems the natural thing to do, making the inclusion of new or underrepresented groups a common part of everyone's agenda. An important line of social research has analyzed the key features of this phenomenon of social climate, identifying those factors that determine whether it promotes strong social bonds and cooperation or whether a social climate is characterized by divisiveness, inequality of respect and resources, suspicion, and defensiveness.

The presence of a civic culture makes the difference. This is a climate characterized by shared expectations that people will behave toward others and other groups in respectful and generally cooperative ways because they believe they can count on those others to treat them in the same way in return. This requires particular individuals and groups to share bonds of trust with those others in their civic community. As we have seen, these relationships are the product of coming together, sharing activities and goals. Civic cultures are distinctive because those bonds extend beyond people who share immediate affinities and similarities. Groups in such cultures not only bond with those like themselves but also actively manage to create relationships that bridge them with groups not like themselves. The key factor is that the members of such societies share a sense of membership in some larger whole. This gives them an ability and willingness to recognize that the well-being of each group depends on cooperation with the others. Such shared expectations and bonds are the prerequisite for a functioning, pluralistic democracy.

Absent a civic culture, the kind of power sharing and compromise on which democratic government depends is likely to break down into deadlock or outright civil conflict.[18]

One great value of a civic culture on campus is that it makes it possible for groups to compromise and to bargain with each other, acknowledging that their interests in some ways diverge but that they can trust the others to bargain in good faith to gain their ends without denying the other groups their ends. As this kind of social climate takes hold, it can grow into a virtuous circle of stronger trust as all groups come to realize that they benefit from cooperating to maintain the larger climate of respect and fairness. While this process may initially depend on taking a risk to trust other groups, over time experience in such environments shows that trust pays off in the form of enhanced well-being in a better overall social climate. Reaching out also depends on ritualized activities that connect and bring others into relationships of respect. Freshman orientation programs, student clubs, and service programs as well as the alumni-student relationships we have noted at a number of NAC&U campuses all exemplify these features of a civic culture on campus. A civic culture in this sense is the aim of every campus community, and, other things being equal, the closer administrators of an institution can come to achieving this sort of climate, the more effective they will likely be at achieving its educational mission.

For students, faculty, and staff, the presence of a civic culture on campus provides the climate in which responsibility and initiative can thrive. One of the most conspicuous effects of civic culture is that it produces in those who participate in it a strong sense of personal efficacy.[19] It is a crucial seedbed for cultivating among students a proactive stance toward their education, strengthening them to take responsibility for their own choices and ambitions for the future. Not surprisingly, therefore, one mark of a strong civic culture on campus is the growth of students' understanding of how to employ their developing knowledge and skills and find a place in the world of work.

Making Something of Oneself: An NAC&U Priority

In a unique large-scale study of the factors that contribute to well-being, or life satisfaction over the long term, Gallup, the nation's pioneering opinion polling firm, in conjunction with Purdue University, has found that the most important single factor was "liking what you do each day and being motivated to achieve your goals," which Gallup calls purpose well-being.[20] Life satisfaction, the Gallup organization has found, has four additional dimensions: strong and supportive relationships and love, economic security, a sense of safety and pride in one's community, and good health. But purpose well-being turns out to be more consistently associated with a happy and fulfilling life than the other dimensions. That means that without purpose well-being, or engagement in work and achieving meaningful goals, it is hard for individuals to feel that their lives are worth living.[21] But if they can achieve this kind of meaningful engagement, they are much more likely to experience the other dimensions of well-being, such as positive relationships, good health, strong community ties, and financial security.

In a survey of more than 30,000 college graduates nationwide, Gallup and Purdue University also discovered that college contributes to developing meaningful purpose and engagement in work by providing three key elements. The first is a professor who cares for the individual as a person and makes him or her excited about learning; the second is a mentor who encourages pursuing large aims beyond college; and the third is an academic project, an internship, or other experience that challenges students to apply what they are learning to practical situations. All these positives go together with being involved in organizations and extracurricular activities.[22] Graduates who reported having had all three factors in their undergraduate experience also reported that they had been well prepared to enter the world of work and career. Those who reported having been excited to learn by caring faculty, having had support in exploring and envisioning future possibilities, and having had experiences where they learned to apply ideas to actual situations were three times more likely to also report high life satisfaction than the average graduate. As the Gallup report summed it up, "Feeling supported and having deep learning experiences means everything when it comes to long-term outcomes for college graduates."[23]

These are the same factors that emerge as the most important for effective college learning as well as what constitutes a positive campus climate. The Gallup findings definitively relate these educational factors to job success and positive life outcomes, illustrating a clear continuity between engaged learning as an undergraduate and achieving a successful life and career as an adult.[24] An NAC&U education that involves learning that integrates liberal arts with professional preparation, provides opportunities for meaningful faculty-student involvement, and supports a campus life marked by civic participation provides the vital matrix for students to develop a proactive stance toward their futures. Such an education is an optimal springboard for exploring possible careers and developing an effective strategy for entering the world of work.

The trend in the NAC&U consortium has been to capitalize on the strengths of the particular campuses to bring career preparation and exploration more deeply into the academic program. Throughout, the aim is to use the educational potentials of various work situations, including on-campus work, to involve students more deeply with their learning and, ultimately, to engage them more thoughtfully and effectively in finding and preparing for their future careers. We have seen several examples of this in the two previous chapters. Manhattan College now uses alumni connections to provide mentors for students who are exploring career possibilities and finding their first jobs. The new core liberal arts program at Nazareth College makes career advising a part of students' experience from the beginning of their college experience. The University of La Verne, whose freshman and sophomore orientation programs were described at the beginning of this chapter, places career considerations before students repeatedly, along with helpful examples and opportunities for mentoring. All NAC&U institutions provide students with many opportunities for this kind of learning.

The Key Career Skill: Learning How to Learn

At the core of all these efforts lies an important kind of learning that has too often been relegated to the sidelines in higher education but remains central to the liberal arts experience as well as genuine professional education. This is learning how to learn for oneself. The essential prerequisite is the ability to know yourself and to use this reflective knowledge to discover and address the purposes of living, including earning a living. A strength of the senior capstone courses we reviewed in Chapter 2 as well as other experiences that ask students to solve problems in actual settings is that they can lead students to retrieve and reframe their learning to better understand the world, similar to laboratory courses in the sciences. Because they lead students to apply concepts to experience, they also open up a reflective dimension in students' thinking. In striving to make sense of the world and formulate and solve problems in experience, students become aware of the power of concepts to clarify the messiness of experience. They can also become aware of the limitations of concepts as concepts provide clarity at the price of simplifying the complexity of experience. We have seen students at several NAC&U campuses make this discovery when struggling with problems of the environment and public health. Through this effort, students become aware, often for the first time, of the intellectual tools they are using to think and to judge their experience and of their dependence on these tools.

Reflective awareness of this kind is one of the most important outcomes of applying ideas to experience. Not only is such reflective thinking one of the most important goals of liberal education; it is also the basis for Gallup's finding about the importance of learning to apply concepts to experience for translating collegiate learning to success in the work world.[25] Courses and counseling that focus on developing this capacity for critical self-reflection, once intentionally connected to questions of purpose, can lead students to be less passive and more proactive in their learning. This proactive attitude can then be extended to using their growing intellectual competence to explore future possibilities for their lives and careers.

With this new awareness, students can make something new of their learning. They can become aware of their own educational process, of how they have come to think the way they do. In other words, self-aware students can reframe their college education to regard it not simply as a set of tasks accomplished or credits earned but as a series of experiences that have helped make them who they are. Students can examine their own experience by asking how a particular program, course, or experience has contributed to their growth as a person. They can also begin to ask about the career potential of the intellectual abilities they have developed as a result of their particular path through college. For example, sociology and anthropology majors might recognize that they have acquired tools of critical analysis of the kind that have important uses in fields such as human resources, consulting, and public service work. Math and science majors may realize they have developed important skills for complex data analysis, abilities very much in demand in a variety of technology jobs in the public and private sectors.

A number of paths lead toward this valuable set of abilities. The proactive stance of self-awareness, the ability to learn on one's own and take responsibility for one's own direction, is the key to being able to make something of oneself in the working world. It is important, however, not to think of this self-awareness as a goal separate from or added on to the core activities of liberal and professional education; rather it is their culmination and completion. Discovering ways to intensify the cultivation of these abilities is being emphasized at NAC&U institutions. The remainder of this chapter focuses on examples such as a work-study program; internships that provide experience in various situations of employment ranging from the corporate world to educational, governmental, health care, and community service settings; and how institutions can offer programs that intentionally emphasize career exploration by integrating it with the other dimensions of an NAC&U education.

Learning Job Skills and More at Hamline University

Hamline University is encouraging students to treat their work-study jobs as important places for learning valuable job skills. As at most colleges and universities, a large number of undergraduates at Hamline receive financial assistance in exchange for part-time work on campus, a national program known as work-study. Certain departments have now instituted ways of bringing work-study students more actively into their academic programs and in the process have made campus work a source of educational growth. One of these departments is theater, which is often an attractive placement for work-study students who have perhaps done theater in high school or find theater work appealing. The theater department at Hamline has reconfigured the way it involves nonmajors to provide them with a better understanding of the business of theater as well as an interesting venue where students can practice and receive feedback on skills they are likely to find useful in the future.

Brittany, a Hamline sophomore, has just attended her first Management Issues meeting. Run by student managers who are theater majors, and monitored by instructors, these meetings are routine and required for all work-study students employed in the various shops run by the theater department. Many of the 45 students employed by the department are, like Brittany, not theater majors. With her fellow box office shop employees, Brittany participates in a discussion of how the student staff handled the problems that arose during the opening night of the theater department's new play. There had been some complaints about the box office on opening night, but Brittany found herself surprised by the directness of the student manager's question: "Why did you refund their money instead of finding them alternative seats?" Brittany struggled to respond, explaining that "their original seats had been given away and there were only single seats left at that point." They were unhappy, Brittany pointed out, "so I gave them the option of sitting apart or getting a refund. They took the refund." A discussion followed, led by the student manager, of the pros and cons of various strategies for dealing with similar situations. In the end, Brittany reported, she felt that she had learned something about how to deal courteously with customers with problems while also making sure that the audience got to their seats on time.

These meetings are important to the effective operation of Hamline's very active theater program. Besides the box office, there are shops for costumes, lighting, makeup, props, scenery, sound, and the TV studio. All are run by student managers under faculty supervision. Meetings to review performance, such as Brittany's box office session, help make the program work, but they are also part of the training that goes with the theater program. Besides performance reviews, shop members such as Brittany get training on how to behave in a job interview, as each shop does its own hiring of work-study students each year, including learning which questions they may legally ask.

The program design is based on a professional employment model, notes theater arts professor Bill Wallace. "Box Office, like the various other shops, has its own work space, job descriptions for its employees, an internal operations guide, and a budget for supplies," he said. All this is part of a deliberate design. Each new student hired must pass a skill test, complete a series of training assessments based on that shop's operations guide, meet the work expectations of their student supervisors, and perform tasks at an expected level of quality. Toward the end of every semester, each student employee must submit a standardized form itemizing his or her achievements (and problems), which is then reviewed and discussed at a performance review session with a student manager and a faculty member in attendance.

Through their work-study time, students like Brittany are not only doing paid work that helps support their academic study but also developing valuable skills for their future careers, regardless of the directions they may later take. Brittany would like a raise, but she has to ask for one, and to get it she must point to value she has added to her shop or to new skills she has developed. After her management meeting, Brittany may be uneasy because of having fumbled a bit on the seating mix-up. However, as Bill Wallace notes in the Hamline program, "It is all right to make mistakes—even the kind that might get you fired in the real world—because faculty advisers are there to help students learn and profit from the experience."

Wallace is underlining one of the important contributions academic settings can make to preparing students for the world of work. While work in real time in actual settings may not allow beginners to learn from making their own mistakes, academic settings can provide students with time offline to practice, receive feedback, analyze, and improve their performance before they have to go online for real. At the next stage, when the academic and the work settings are coordinated, students can begin to move from the role of learner to actively adding value in the world. This is the pedagogical achievement of internship and placement.[26]

Internship to First Job to Graduate Degree at The Sage Colleges

Supervised placement or internship in a professional or work setting can be one of the most educationally valuable steps toward finding a future career. In Chapter 1, for example, we saw how clinical psychology students benefited from volunteer placements as part of their studies at the University of Redlands; in Chapter 2 Manhattan College's alumni mentor program helped students explore meaningful employment. Also in Chapter 2, Valparaiso University meteorology students discussed experiencing the life of practicing scientists, Ohio Northern University's business senior capstone introduced undergraduates to actual business clients in responsible roles, and Pacific Lutheran University made use of internships as part of its senior capstone experience. All NAC&U institutions offer internships, many conferring academic credit and directly connected to the student's major. These internship and placement programs provide dramatic illustrations of the factors various studies on success in college have singled out, especially a strongly engaged faculty and a positive campus climate.

For example, David McCarty transferred to the Sage College of Albany as a junior and in the process changed his major from engineering to business administration. David reported having struggled at several other institutions while trying to find direction in his first two years of college. For David, the Sage College was "finding the right fit." As he put it, "Once at Sage College Albany, the enthusiasm and support of the professors (particularly Professor Ko, Dr. Fredericks, and Professor Brownell) drove me to do my best to get exceptional grades; anything less and I felt I'd be letting everyone down."

David noted that the professors at Sage "really formed connections with students. I could tell they were passionate about student learning. That, in turn, made me passionate about wanting to 'excel.'" He concluded that coming to Sage was "the best decision I've made for my collegiate career as well as for the future."

As part of his degree program, David became an intern in 2013, working at Gavant Software in Troy, New York. In that placement he was able "to see firsthand the interest in the project [he was] working on, as well as actually seeing a visual representation of what the app [he] was working on would look like." The internship provided David with the opportunity to become actively involved in product design by suggesting to his supervisor several visual and functional concepts from other apps David had studied on his own. As he put it,

> It was awesome to see my research of competing apps being used to create a product for our company. Being told you're doing a good job is one thing, but actually seeing that your boss values your work by incorporating some of your ideas into a project is exceptionally rewarding.

Upon completion of his formal internship, Gavant Software hired David as a part-time employee during his senior year. His work included a focus on new product development, which encompassed market research, competitive analysis, and Web and social media marketing. His efforts yielded positive customer feedback on the mobile app he had helped design. David's contributions were recognized by the Center for Economic

Growth's Technology Innovation Award, which is presented to the most innovative and growth-oriented companies and individuals in the Albany area's Tech Valley. Convinced he has found the match between his skills, interests, and bettering the world, David since graduation has decided to pursue an advanced degree and is now enrolled in the Sage MBA program at Albany.[27]

Learning to Network and Improve the World at Wagner College

Wagner College embodies another feature typical of NAC&U institutions: It is deeply connected with its neighboring communities and its region. In Wagner's case, its location on Staten Island, a borough of New York City connected to Manhattan by ferry and Brooklyn by bridge, provides striking opportunities for students to combine learning through supervised experience with formal classroom teaching. Wagner has developed a large number of internship positions in a range of New York City institutions, ranging from the performing arts to Wall Street to government and nonprofit organizations, such as the Clinton Foundation in New York City.

During his senior year, Chris De Filippi, a government and politics major, dressed up and headed to Manhattan from his Staten Island home by express bus three days a week to the office of the Bill, Hillary & Chelsea Clinton Foundation on 125th Street in Harlem. A large international nonprofit founded by President Bill Clinton, the Clinton Foundation employs about 65 interns at its offices and initiatives in New York City. Chris was placed in the scheduling department, a position so sensitive that he was not allowed to disclose any details of his work.

As Chris pointed out, "It was a once-in-a-lifetime opportunity to work for a former president." Besides doing a steady stream of scheduling work in the office, he had the opportunity to attend special events, such as the closing ceremonies of the latest Clinton Global Initiative meeting, featuring speeches by Bill, Hillary, and Chelsea Clinton, and a seminar with the former president held especially for the interns. Chris views this internship as an important training ground for his career path. "I wanted to take what I've learned [at Wagner]—leadership skills, communication skills—and apply them to a nonprofit. The Clinton Foundation is the biggest nonprofit in New York City."

Back on campus, Chris attended his senior learning community's capstone seminar and reflective tutorial, where his fellow senior majors in government and politics as well as international affairs discussed their internships and worked on their senior theses. He wrote about the garment industry in Bangladesh compared with sweatshops in New York City and Milan, where he studied abroad the year before. As Chris put it,

That's what I like about Wagner. Through my internship and also from study abroad, I found out there's a lot that could be done in the nonprofit sector, and it could bring about great change, with more and more people getting involved.

The evolution of Chris's interest in nonprofits started in his first-year learning community, which focused on dissenting voices in literature and politics. A large Liberian community lives near the Wagner campus, inspiring Chris to read Liberian literature and work at African Refuge, a community-based organization dedicated to helping refugees. As a sophomore, he took Feminist Political Theory with Patricia Moynagh. The seminar-style, discussion-driven class was so engaging, and the ideas so inspiring, that he has made the women's equality movement his personal focus. As a gay man who had recently come out, he identified with women's struggles to gain a voice in society. To that end, he has been working this semester for another nonprofit organization with ongoing connections to Wagner College. At the women's leadership organization Take the Lead, Chris has built up the group's social media presence. "That's what I do in my spare time—the very little I seem to have," he said wryly.[28]

Bridging College and Career at the University of Evansville

At the University of Evansville in Indiana some internships are part of an integrated program called GAP. Begun by the university's Schroeder School of Business, this program organizes teams of students from across the university to work for various kinds of enterprise, including government, for-profit, and non-profit organizations. The students apply what they are learning on campus to assist these organizations with the problems and issues they face in our more globally connected world. GAP has built on the existing strengths of Evansville's liberal arts and professional schools to produce "adaptive learners." Like The Sage Colleges and Wagner, Evansville has put its long history of strong relationships with the Evansville area to use to make the program effective.

GAP offers students a variety of ways to learn by putting their academic skills into action to solve problems for these organizations. With more than 10 years of experience in 75 projects, some of which have continued from year to year, the program often involves Indiana companies and organizations working in collaboration with "enterprise partners" in various parts of the world. These interactions provide rich environments in which students can learn not only how to put their knowledge into practice but also where they can develop the important skills of critical thinking, oral and written communication, leadership, and personal and team responsibility.

Coached by participating faculty, Evansville students are working to improve the inventory system at a health clinic in rural Guatemala, a matter of considerable value to the overstretched clinic in a poor area of the country. The project team is made up of students who bring insights and skills from a variety of majors: exercise/physical therapy, accounting, neuroscience, nursing, public health administration, global business, languages, and international studies. Student interns are introduced to the subtleties of intercultural work and the pressures of global business and politics through their work with firms and organizations in Indiana and in Guatemala. The student benefit in this, as in other GAP projects, is that their internship experience can lead to connections in unexpected and positive directions.

One of GAP's ongoing partners is a local Evansville start-up, Curvo Labs, which develops sourcing platforms to link medical device suppliers directly with hospitals and clinics. The opportunity to work on GAP projects such as the one involving the Guatemala clinic has provided Richy Ludwick, an Evansville senior, with an eye-opening exposure to the global career opportunities his major in public health administration is preparing him for. "Working with Curvo has shown me that it's possible for great things to come out of Indiana!" he said. A GAP alumnus with the same major and similar experience, David Work, was recently hired by Curvo as a full-time account manager. "As a health administration major, a lot of the opportunities are more prevalent in the big cities with larger health systems," David said. "So, having the opportunity to work in my field with an innovative company while also staying in Evansville is a great opportunity." Curvo Labs cofounder Andy Perry commented, "Curvo was fortunate to have had the work of the program and the talent of the students on our project. Thanks so much!"

The professional connections made available by GAP internships can be especially valuable, and sometimes surprising, for students in majors other than business or the health fields. Whitney Darret, another recent alumna of the program, majored in German and international studies. Her GAP experience led directly to her being hired as a project manager for IBM Global Business Services. "I credit much of my success to the GAP program," Whitney stated, "and the two leading professors on my project. During my later job interviews and the sending of quick follow-up e-mails, I thought back on the GAP program's demands and realized I was prepared!" Whitney noted that "IBM was extremely interested in what I reported about GAP and was impressed by what I was able to show and tell them about what I learned there." Christine Mueller, a creative writing major who participated in a GAP project in her senior year, was equally enthusiastic:

> The day we presented our research was one of the highlights of my undergraduate experience, and the sense of accomplishment I felt gave me con-

fidence in my professional skills and abilities. . . . We were finding a real solution for a real company.

The perspectives of liberal learning that the Evansville students brought to their GAP intern experiences were noteworthy to their enterprise partners as well. (Regardless of their majors, they were all veterans of the university's extensive liberal arts core program.) The broad multidisciplinary viewpoint the students brought was appreciated by people at the organizations they worked for. Randy Hobson, vice president for commercial development of Berry Plastics of Indiana, judged participation in the GAP program as "a really great experience for our company that provided an opportunity to engage with a diverse group of students." Hobson went on to note that "the multidisciplinary team had a comprehensive approach. . . . Their delivery was first class. It certainly exceeded our expectations. The team garnered new ideas, new thoughts, new perceptions that we just wouldn't have seen otherwise." It is needless to add that few of the students who took part in the GAP program with Berry Plastics had to be convinced that a liberal arts education provided practical benefits for life and work, as well as comprehensive understanding.[29]

Conclusion: Campus Climate Spurs Learning for Success

A positive campus climate provides the ground for students to flourish in college. This chapter presents a variety of examples of programs at NAC&U campuses that are designed to achieve these goals. Learning and personal growth depend on a campus climate of respect, inclusion, and trust in which academic expectations are high and students are challenged and supported.

This kind of positive campus climate also provides students with the motivation and the tools to achieve their ambitions to make something of themselves. Exploring possibilities for meaningful employment after graduation and preparing to enter the working world are important priorities of an NAC&U education. This chapter illustrates how various institutions are able to productively align academic learning and experience with professional work through internships and placements that draw on the strengths of the campus and the workplace. Graduates' as well as current students' testimony on the effectiveness of these programs in enabling students to find the right fit among their interests and hopes, their abilities, and the needs of the larger society and the world reveal the enormous positive potential that life and learning in a vital campus community offer students at NAC&U campuses.

Notes

1. Public Affairs Office, Belmont University, personal communication, August 3, 2014.

2. St. Edward's University, personal communication, February 6, 2015.

3. Pascarella, Terenzini, & Wolfe, "Orientation to College and Freshman Year Persistence/Withdrawal Decisions"; see also Tinto, *Leaving College*.

4. Tinto, *Leaving College*; Pascarella & Terenzini, *How College Affects Students*.

5. Blaich, *How Do Students Change Over Four Years of College?*; Arum & Roksa, *Academically Adrift*; Arum & Roksa, *Aspiring Adults Adrift*.

6. Astin, *What Matters in College*.

7. Ibid.; Light, *Getting the Most Out of College*.

8. Clydesdale, *The Purposeful Graduate*.

9. Chambliss & Takacs, *How College Works*, p. 132.

10. Ibid., p. 112.

11. Ibid., pp. 132–133.

12. Ibid., p. 132.

13. Kuh, Schuh, Whitt, & Associates, *Involving Colleges*.

14. Chambliss & Takacs, *How College Works*.

15. S. Varhus, personal communication, February 10, 2015.

16. McNeill, *Keeping Together in Time*; on the power of rituals of bonding, see also Collins, *Interaction Ritual Chains*.

17. Chambliss & Takacs, *How College Works*, p. 4.

18. This idea of civic culture as characterized by bridging social norms and expanding networks of cooperation and trust has been developed by political scientist Robert C. Putnam; Putnam, *Bowling Alone*; see also Putnam, *Our Kids*, his analysis of the destructive effects of the growing socioeconomic inequality on American youths.

19. This is a theme in Robert Putnam's research, as noted in note 18; see also Almond & Verba, *The Civic Culture*.

20. Gallup & Purdue University, *Great Jobs Great Lives*, p. 3.

21. Ibid., p. 7.

22. Ibid.

23. Ibid., p. 6.

24. Gallup & Purdue University, *Great Jobs Great Lives*.

25. Ibid.

26. B. Wallace, personal communication, September 5, 2014.

27. E. V. Brownwell, personal communication, August 4, 2014.

28. L. Barlament, "Starting a Career Path"; personal communication, May 2014.

29. J. Griffin, personal communication, March 5, 2015.

4

BECOMING A CITIZEN AND ENGAGING WITH THE WORLD

The previous chapter presents some of the emerging programs NAC&Us are using to help students connect their developing academic abilities with their personal growth as well as their preparation for the demands of the workplace. The critical factor for this turned out to be the strength and vitality of campus community. This chapter follows this insight to explore how NAC&U's strong campus cultures enable students to integrate their academic learning with career preparation and personal development while performing service to others through citizenship in communities, their profession, the nation, and the world. It presents examples, often featuring student voices, from a number of campuses that show the variety of approaches to fostering civic commitment ranging from academic courses that emphasize learning in service and partnership with communities, to campus-community partnerships, and study opportunities designed to promote a sense of global citizenship and responsibility for the environment.

Educating for civic responsibility is deeply embedded in the identity of American higher education. The charters of many colleges and universities, public and private, state that the education of citizens is an essential and defining mission of higher education in the United States.[1] Preparation for democratic citizenship is also endorsed as a goal of college learning by many of the traditions of religious faith that are integral to a significant segment of higher education.[2] NAC&U campuses are outstanding in the attention they give to expressing in innovative ways higher education's civic mission to be relevant to today's students. This chapter shows how educating for civic responsibility can function as one of the most powerful means of fostering the growth of purpose in young lives, a purpose that can engage and fulfill the self while also integrating people into relationships and goals that transcend the individual.

Nurturing an Orientation to Service at the University of Scranton

The University of Scranton in northeastern Pennsylvania describes its mission as an expression of its Catholic and Jesuit tradition of providing students with ways to connect their learning with experience and practice. The university's Leahy Community Health and Family Center is dedicated to the dual purpose of identifying and meeting the health and wellness needs of underserved individuals in the greater Scranton community while also providing a place where faculty can guide students in a practical educational experience focused on service to the university's neighbors.

In their orientation experience, and later through academic courses that include components in which students participate in community service and then reflect on the meaning of their experiences, Scranton students are introduced to the university's commitment to the Jesuit mission of educating "men and women for others." The center provides a way for students to continue to explore this aspect of their college experience with a particular focus on the health fields. It presents students with a lived experience of what it means to call fields such as nursing, medicine, and physical therapy "helping professions."

The center is also an example of the university's deep engagement in the Scranton community. It is widely recognized as a place where the marginalized and underserved population of the city and region can benefit from high-quality health, wellness, and education services delivered with respect and care. Although it provides valuable clinical experience for majors in the health fields, it also enables students in other fields to gain firsthand experience of serving the marginalized in a well-organized and carefully supervised context. Students from all parts of the undergraduate population work closely with faculty, professional staff, and fellow students at the center.

Since its beginning a decade ago, the Leahy Community Health and Family Center has grown to include programs and services that advance the educational and research mission of the university while providing vital services to communities in northeastern Pennsylvania. This means that students get to work in a variety of health care contexts, such as a clinic for the uninsured (the first free clinic in the county), a food and clothing pantry, occupational and physical therapy services, and a counseling clinic, among others. This wide range of services is possible through the university's commitment and the dedication of professionals who volunteer at the center—physicians, nurse practitioners, and nurses from around the Scranton area—whose work, along with that of university faculty and staff, provides a powerful example of the meaning of an orientation to service. The center's activities visibly build up the larger community outside the university, while students quickly come to realize that their work too is needed and that it matters.

For Scranton students, time at the Leahy center interweaves learning and service in very forceful ways, often sparking or intensifying students' long-term commitment to service in the growing health care fields. For other students, such as education majors, work at the center can shape their own sense of efficacy, showing them that they can make a difference in the lives of others and that they need to learn to have as much positive effect as they can.

Cara Brindley, a 2012 graduate, was a nursing major and while pursuing her degree served as a student volunteer coordinator at the center for several academic years while also doing some of her clinical training there. While working at the clinic for the uninsured, Cara was part of a team that treated an older patient suffering from a cough. The nurse practitioner in charge diagnosed his condition as acute bronchitis and advised him of the steps necessary for recovery. The patient replied that he would have trouble complying because he was presently homeless and living in a damp box. Furthermore, he had already spent the money he had saved up on an incorrect medication. Cara and another student nurse tried to persuade him to accept referral to a shelter. When he refused, fearing theft of his few possessions, Cara realized that she and the staff would have to improvise if they were to provide the care this patient needed.

Collectively the staff decided to provide the man with the correct medication free of charge along with warmer clothing, a jacket, and some pre-packaged food from the center's pantry. They invited him to return soon afterward for follow-up care, which he did. For Cara, the incident became an important educational moment. She reported that she learned that health care can and sometimes must mean more than simply adhering to expected procedures. It requires thinking of the patient as a full person and working collectively, and creatively if need be, to meet that person's needs. By her testimony, this experience made the university's ideal of becoming "men and women for others" concrete and something to be lived out day by day through her life as a student nurse. It provided an awareness of what it meant to be responsible for the well-being of others.[3]

An NAC&U Hallmark

The programs at the University of Scranton described in this chapter, and those at John Carroll University described in Chapter 1, are distinctive but not unique in the NAC&U consortium with its mission of providing an education that "integrates liberal arts, professional studies, and civic responsibility." From the beginning of this book, we have seen examples of how this integration is played out on different campuses of the consortium. The programs and courses we have examined are conspicuous for their use of educational practices known to have high impacts on student learning. This is equally true for the third part of the mission: developing a sense of civic understanding and engagement as an expression of the purpose of higher education in a democratic society.

This has been a distinctly American feature of the NAC&U movement from its inception. In 1995 the founders of the consortium were inspired by civic idealism. Boyer described one of the organization's key aims as a commitment to community on campus but as a value of great importance to American democracy as well.[4] Since its inception, the NAC&U has demonstrated a high level of commitment to preparing students for lives of engagement in the communities and times in which they live.

This commitment is evident on all NAC&U campuses and takes a number of characteristic forms. The most widespread is offering academic courses in the liberal arts and professional studies that involve direct experience with work and research beyond the campus to enhance the civic life of the larger communities of the college or university. In addition, a number of campuses also operate centers in the community that provide valuable services in areas ranging from business development to health care to environmental protection. At these centers students can learn how to integrate various bodies of academic knowledge with specific civic skills, such as participation in mutual dialogue, deliberation, and work to achieve common aims.

These experiences often involve students working with teams that unite a variety of points of view and expertise. Internships and time spent working in community organizations under the direction of faculty and partners in the community, often incorporated as senior capstone experiences and sometimes with career services, is also an area for students to explore the dimensions of civic life. In these experiences, they discover the reward of civic participation and the challenge to develop ways to persevere through conflict and difficulty.

By weaving civic themes and questions through these experiences, NAC&U campuses provide motivation for engaged reflection and growth in personal and ethical understanding. They fill out and give substance to the aims of liberal education. Through integrating students' learning from a variety of areas, these encounters with civic life provide a larger horizon for students to develop their professional skills. The most important contribution of the civic dimension, perhaps, is that it expands students' sense of their own efficacy as participants in the larger world. Particularly for students who come from backgrounds in which social efficacy cannot be taken for granted, this is particularly valuable in preparing them for making a successful life beyond college.

NAC&U's emphasis on the civic vision of what college can be and do for students makes it a particular source of hope and encouragement in higher education as a whole. In a time of uncertainty about older expectations about ways to succeed in life and inherited assumptions about life after college, thoughtful critics of higher education have noted that colleges often do too little to address what Andrew Delbanco calls "this siege of uncertainty." What is too often missing or pushed to the sidelines, argues Delbanco, is that

> one of the insights at the core of the college idea—indeed of the idea of community itself—has always been that to serve others is to serve oneself by providing a sense of purpose, thereby countering the loneliness and aimlessness by which all people, young and old, can be afflicted.[5]

Whatever the truth of this accusation for higher education as a whole, the NAC&U institutions as a group provide powerful proof that it is possible to do better.

The institutions profiled here are not developing their innovative forms of civic education in isolation but are active participants in movements seeking to strengthen the civic focus of the college experience. The University of Scranton and John Carroll University share a set of common values with other universities and colleges of the worldwide network of Jesuit institutions of higher learning. Both are also active members of a national organization known as the Network for Values in Undergraduate Education (NetVUE). Now a program of the Council of Independent Colleges, NetVUE focuses on students' exploration of vocation or calling. NetVUE campuses provide a variety of ways for students to begin to explicitly deal with questions about their sense of purpose, their interests and capacities, and how they can organize their college experience to answer the question of what they might do with their lives.[6]

In keeping with these goals, a number of NAC&U institutions, such as John Carroll University, the University of La Verne, and the University of Scranton, have placed increased emphasis on such questions, introducing them at the beginning of orientation for new students. Framing questions about personal aspiration in relation to the needs of the larger world encourages students, even beginning students, to consider how their aims might figure within a greater whole. And for their part, many students find this emphasis a valuable way to make sense of their own educational aspirations. The several hundred institutions that make up NetVUE go about this in different ways, but they move questions of life purpose from the periphery to the center of students' experience in college, which can be enlivening and enriching for young lives. In addition to John Carroll and the University of La Verne, North Central College, Ohio Northern University, Pacific Lutheran University, St. Edward's University, Samford University, University of Scranton, Valparaiso University, and Wagner College all participate in NetVUE.[7]

Educating Citizens: The Contours of a Civic Self

In New York's Central Park, one of the great monuments to American civic spirit, a marble bench bears the following inscription: *Alteri vivere oportet si tibi vis vivere.* (If you want to live for yourself, you must live for others.) It summarizes the sense of public spirit that Central Park embodies and that democracy depends on. The NAC&U commitment to civic education extends these long-standing American values to fostering in their graduates an interest in what affects the public, especially how their choices and decisions affect the lives of others.

A democratic nation requires its members to think of themselves and experience themselves as citizens. These people share the belief that governing their communities and their society as a whole is their own concern. Claiming and exercising these rights of participation provides individuals with what Martin Luther King Jr. called a sense of "somebodiness," the dignity that is the promise of democratic citizenship. Working to secure and exercise those rights generates the power to act and accomplish goals together. The resulting sense of efficacy is an important dimension of freedom. Strong, inclusive civic cultures of this type have been rare in history, and the achievement of a fully democratic way of life is still far from complete anywhere. The United States is today facing many serious problems as a nation and a society. It suffers from gross socioeconomic inequality, racial and religious divisions, controversy over the integration of immigrants, and has great difficulty in grappling with the effects of environmental degradation. Yet, as past and present examples illustrate, mutual trust and responsibility among citizens make problems solvable. They provide the necessary bedrock for justice, cooperation, and the respect for the rule of law that mark a democratic society. If the civic mission of higher education is to foster such a culture of citizenship, it has surely never mattered more.

This is the challenge the NAC&U's founders urged their member institutions to take on. They also recognized, however, that they could draw on the resources of a long and powerful American tradition of civic cooperation. It is worth recalling the particular logic of this tradition, a way of organizing society that Americans often take for granted but that has often struck thoughtful visitors from other lands. The first of these was French citizen Alexis de Tocqueville, who visited the new United States before the Civil War and recorded his assessment of what he saw in a now famous work he titled *Democracy in America.* Tocqueville was no naive optimist. He warned that the nation faced two large obstacles to its democratic development: the "relations among the races" and the possibility of a new kind of economic tyranny based on large-scale industrial technology. However, he located America's future as a democracy in the nation's ability to employ its civic commitments to overcome the real obstacles he discerned.

Tocqueville found the most salient feature of American life was what he called "individualism." He distinguished individualism from personal self-ishness by calling it a "calm and considered feeling," what today would be called a shared cultural value or trait,

> which disposes each citizen to isolate himself from the mass of his fellows and withdraw into the circle of family and friends. With this little society formed after his taste, he gladly leaves the larger society to look after itself.[8]

According to Tocqueville, in such a society, where individuals pursued individual economic success as a major goal, their understandable desire to be independent and self-sufficient also carried potentially negative consequences.

> Such folk form the habit of thinking of themselves in isolation and imagine that their whole destiny is in their hands. . . . Each is forever thrown back on his own self and there is danger that each may be shut up in the solitude of his own heart.[9]

In short, Tocqueville had discovered in competitive individualism the default mode of the American cultural operating system, and this was before personal communication devices, iPods, or even TV.[10]

Guided by his diagnosis of the American context, Tocqueville was particularly attentive to those institutions and practices Americans learned to use to overcome the negative consequences of individualism, or, as he put it, how they "combat individualism by means of the doctrine of self-interest rightly understood."[11] The key, he thought, was that the relatively decentralized nature of their federal republic obliged Americans "to take part in public affairs" in a variety of ways: serving on juries and commissions, organizing to pass legislation, and forming committees and organizations on particular interests and larger scale causes.[12] (Tocqueville was in the United States during the period of antislavery agitation, among other national causes.) He also saw the Americans of his time cooperating to form religious organizations, schools, and clubs as well as involving themselves in public affairs on a wide range of topics.

The positive effect, Tocqueville noted, was that in these involvements "they must turn from their private interests and occasionally take a look at something other than themselves."[13] He emphasized that "Americans of all ages, all stations in life, and all types of dispositions are forever forming associations."[14] There, they learned how to listen, speak, and deliberate together. If they were to succeed in their undertakings, they also had to learn how to compromise and cooperate. Although Americans usually said it was "self-interest" that drew them into these activities, Tocqueville noted that such participation gradually shaped civic dispositions, even fostering a taste for serving their neighbors. This self-interest was rightly understood—individuals willingly surrendered some of their time and energy to common projects and received in return an enhanced sense of self and a wider range of ideas and connections.[15] To this French observer, the vibrant civic culture that resulted was cause for hope about the American future.

In Tocqueville's perspective, participation in democratic institutions was educational in the deep sense: It formed civic-minded people. This is the same insight that has guided the development of programs in civic engagement at NAC&U campuses. Civic life, over time, changes and enlarges the person who takes part in it. It can provide an orientation in life, making it possible for individuals to develop their abilities in ways that open up the unique kind of self-fulfillment Tocqueville thought he observed at work in American life. A civic orientation focuses attention on involvement with others, other generations and other kinds of people whose differences the process of working together on common projects can reveal as valuable assets for the whole upon which each individual's well-being finally depends.

Civic Engagement as a Platform for Integrating Undergraduate Education

Civic education is a natural companion to liberal learning. It provides a practical basis for the intellectual activity of making sense of others and the world. To understand another person, society, time, or way of living requires the effort to go beyond one's own boundaries. Understanding others requires a will to understand; however, understanding others is also a learned ability, the skill of interpreting, that is cultivated by liberal education. But the very process of interpretation is potentially a social action, reaching out to the other, a willingness to be affected by the other. This is the process at work in all human relationships, linking the personal to the social and political. Successful interpretation makes familiar what was at first incomprehensible or strange, and, by doing so, builds new connections with the other. Out of these connections with their new understandings, common purposes often emerge.

This deeply practical dimension of liberal learning becomes immediately visible when the learning takes place in situations that allow the learners to recognize differences and similarities in the other. As this happens, the interpreter grows in self-awareness. When this process of making sense of the other's perspective is reciprocated, when communication is established, a new or deepened relationship becomes possible. Expansion and deepening of a relationship does more than expand awareness. It also strengthens the sense of agency of all involved. That is why growth in engagements of this kind provides a continuous motivation for further learning, which spurs further engagement. This virtuous cycle that unites intellectual with personal growth is the dynamic structure that makes experiential learning a high-impact practice often prized by students.

The key to college success, positive student-faculty relationships, derives its motivational power from the same process. When civic education is done well, it often incorporates strong student-faculty interaction and experiential learning, providing an ideal platform for supporting integrated learning. We have seen this in a number of examples throughout this book. A campus or a program administrator whose goal is that students be able to synthesize their academic learning with their social experiences in a personally meaningful way, gains valuable relationships through civic partnerships that extend beyond the campus. These relationships then contribute to the educational power of the campus even as they extend the horizon of the campus culture, as we have also seen. A civically oriented campus culture in turn leads students to imagine purposeful ways to use their knowledge and skills in the future to extend the goals and connections they have begun to experience in college.

Since the education of a civic orientation is a living process, it has to be renewed in each generation. Its forms and modes must likewise be able to change to fit new circumstances. Although present circumstances may not be any more daunting than those Tocqueville saw Americans facing in the nineteenth century, they are new and challenging. Today's students and faculty also live in a society that has many forces, some pressures, and other attractions, which if unopposed would lead the individual "to isolate himself from the mass of his fellows and withdraw into the circle of family and friends . . . [and then] gladly leave the larger society to look after itself."[16] It is for this reason that part of the educational mission of NAC&U campuses requires them to provide their students with appealing opportunities to grow in their understanding of and commitment to a civic identity.

Sustainability and Global Awareness at North Central College

A civic identity means that a person acknowledges that concern for the welfare of the larger world is part of his or her deepest purposes. Updating Tocqueville's insight, the essential spirit of democratic living must surely include people all around the globe as well as the welfare of the natural environment in that range of concern.[17] Although officials at many colleges and universities talk about educating students to change or improve the world, especially the environment, few have tried more comprehensively to infuse that perspective into their curriculum and campus culture than North Central College in Naperville, Illinois. North Central has emerged as a leader in committing to a sustainable world as well as introducing students to the complexities of human social relationships on a global scale.

In its plan for use of its land and natural resources, North Central explicitly links achieving a more sustainable campus environment to its aim to support learning and attract students and faculty who share North Central's values and environmental commitments. To make all this more actual on a day-to-day basis, North Central has established a campuswide sustainability committee, recruiting its members from students as well as faculty and administrative staff. The committee's charge is to involve the entire campus community, and the college's partners in the Chicago metropolitan area, in programs and action with the goal of making use of new technologies and changing patterns of living to support long-range sustainability.

North Central's president, Troy D. Hammond, is a scientifically trained technologist who has presented his college's approach in a TEDx Talk titled "Sustainability: Why Universities Can Lead by Example," in which he described how the college will invest a portion of its endowment funds in more efficient lighting, energy, and transportation projects. Such endowment-based "green funds," argued Hammond, hold great future potential:

> A college like North Central has the time horizon to experience the full upside and benefit of energy efficiency projects . . . and the expertise to evaluate these projects, to assess the science behind the technology, to model the energy, to evaluate the financials, to verify the math.

In other words, by leveraging the liberal arts, together with professional expertise, higher education institutions can make a large public contribution in an area critical for the world's future. If North Central's model proves successful and catches on, it could be used by the nation's colleges and universities to make a significant reduction in the carbon footprint of the nation as a whole.

Similar ideas animate the college's new major in environmental studies. One of the first students in the program, Jackie, is also president of Green Scene, a student organization that spreads ideas about practices and technologies that support a sustainable future. "Life is about finding a balance, and North Central offers a great balance between classroom learning and real-world experience," Jackie noted, recommending North Central to "anyone who prefers a hands-on approach to learning." She confided, "I learned more by interning with the campus sustainability coordinator and talking one-on-one with professors than I would have learned sitting in a lecture hall at a large school." In her cocurricular activities as well as in her major program, Jackie gives personal affirmation to the college's commitment to making positive change in the way Americans currently relate to their environment. This is surely an important aspect of civic engagement for the twenty-first century.[18]

The Global Scale of Civic Learning at North Central

North Central also has a record of providing students with the means and inspiration to engage in civic learning on a global scale. Through its Office of Ministry and Service, the college sponsors immersion trips that bring North Central students into contact with people and situations with pressing issues of conflict, peace, and justice. One of the most memorable of these was a two-week immersion trip to the Middle East taken by a group of 10 students led by a staff team from the Office of Ministry and Service. While in Israel and the West Bank, students spent about equal time with Palestinians and Israelis, visiting 10 different sites. The educational aim was to develop skills in analyzing and evaluating complex information from multiple, often conflicting perspectives in tense environments marked by sharp contrasts and opposed positions. The expectation was that students would engage throughout the trip in group and individual reflection and that students would perceive the value of building bridges of mutual understanding. Students could discover the real-world value of the ideals of justice and reconciliation, leading to some later form of civic action based on the enhanced civic knowledge they would acquire from the experience.

Because of its intensity, the trip required students to commit to four months of regular study sessions in advance, focused on the history of the people and groups they would encounter, analyzing these factors for their impact of ethnicity, religion, and citizenship on everyday life. Once in Israel, the students spent their days meeting and talking with Israelis and Palestinians in a variety of settings. They were expected to apply theoretical perspectives to their experiences, which led to intense learning as students were challenged to evaluate the Israeli-Palestinian situation from multiple sources, inquiring into the role of the United States in the peace process and raising the question of what responsibility, if any, they might have personally for communicating or acting on what they were learning. Themes of conflict resolution loomed large for a number of the students. And as in any intense involvement, the situation built deeper relationships among the participants as well as with those they encountered and came to know as they traveled.

Following the immersion experience, and after a debriefing, students wrote their reflections. But perhaps most significantly, a number of students went on to take significant action in light of their time in the Middle East. One has worked with a small Palestinian organization to develop a proposal for a grant to bring conflict resolution and children's books to a community center in a West Bank village. Another decided to write her honors thesis on water in the region and its effects on the current situation. Yet another developed his own study program in Israel to continue to explore issues first introduced by the immersion trip. Many of the aspirations of the organizers were thus fulfilled. As an unexpected benefit, administrators and staff and North Central were able to learn more about how to make use of the intensity generated in carefully organized encounters with actual social complexity to inspire deep, engaged learning that enables students to grow into mature citizens of their nation and the world.[19]

What the Research Shows, Illustrated by NAC&U Examples

To support students toward such an ambitious goal as becoming active citizens of their world, the campus culture is a primary resource. The importance of achieving the goal of civic engagement justifies institutions' often considerable investments of personnel and resources in nurturing such an atmosphere in all sectors of the campus community. As we saw in the previous chapter, cultivating a strong, civically oriented campus climate is one of the most powerful resources that enable students to succeed academically, personally, and in the workplace. Beyond and including this, the civic orientation of a campus bears out the NAC&U founders' belief that a college community whose daily way of living inculcates concern for the dignity of others and recognizes their mutual interdependence within a wider ecology would be able to guide students toward integrating for themselves yet together with others the multiple facets of their growth into a life marked by curiosity, resilience, and a concern with the larger community.

Studies of successful programs that inspire and sustain civic engagement share certain characteristics. Most important, they are not add-ons but enact and reinforce teaching in the curriculum and cocurriculum. Through "habitual participation in practices, routines, and communal events," members of the campus community develop a "shared culture" that "has the power to shape the frameworks through which future experiences are interpreted."[20] Service-learning experiences, when they are made subjects of reflection in courses, are high-impact practices, and so are internships and placements in organizations that are involved with social service and civic and political life as well as curricular learning communities and culminating projects.[21] In addition, successful programs seek to cultivate the kind of reciprocal understanding of self and others that makes it possible for individuals to interact with difference and weave ties of connection among various groups and cultures. Examples range from community involvement to solving common practical problems to interfaith dialogues. Lively debate, sometimes impassioned, about the meaning of a culture's values and their implications is a mark of a vital culture.

In other words, the research points to the value of using experiential learning and relationships with community partners beyond the campus to engage students' interest in learning.[22] In Chapter 1 we saw an example of this with the Wagner College learning community, Living on Spaceship Earth, that focused on work with community partners in Northern New Jersey around issues of environmental sustainability. This pedagogy makes it possible to encourage students to employ some of the energy that results toward exploring ways to address what they come to perceive as important although sometimes difficult problems. The experience of North Central College, with its sustainability initiative and its programs that provide learning labs for global citizenship, is hopeful in this regard. Next, we consider another example of the creative possibilities for learning and maturity that can be generated when civic partnerships are linked to academic learning.

Widener University's Journalism Students and *Chester*

Widener University is located close to Chester, Pennsylvania, a small city on the Delaware River that was once a bustling industrial port and center. Its proud motto, "What Chester Makes, Makes Chester," reflects that history and is still displayed on an electric sign visible along the busy rails of the Northeast Corridor. Unfortunately, and for some time, the city suffered the ills of many once prosperous industrial centers. So it is encouraging to hear the city's former mayor, John Linder, himself a major factor in trying to turn Chester around, talking about being "excited about the future of the city." He was speaking about the launch of a new magazine called *Chester*, whose first issue included a photo essay about the city, emphasizing its recent development efforts through public-private partnerships, profiles of the Chester Children's Chorus, staff at the Crozier-Chester Medical Center, various Chester bakeries and restaurants, and a story about the city's plans for a cultural corridor.

The magazine is unusual because it is entirely the work of students at Widener University with a number of community partners in the city. *Chester* grew out of Magazine Journalism, a course taught in the spring of 2014 by Sam Starnes, who also edits Widener's campus magazine, among his other functions for the university. One of the new magazine's columnists, Khalil Williams, grew up in Chester. "I feel Chester has the potential to grow," he wrote, "because there are people who are passionate and interested in seeing the city be better. . . . I feel that it can be full of life again." Certainly, Khalil and his fellow students in that journalism course have been infected by a sense of hope for the city.

The magazine is a tangible outgrowth of the enthusiasm and developing competence of the students in Starnes's class. But it couldn't have happened without the supporting relationship between the university and the community, connections that Widener has woven carefully over the course of decades. As Linder has emphasized, the university has proven itself a trustworthy partner. The campus culture is highly supportive of projects such as the magazine and in fact actively promotes such endeavors. The magazine project was underwritten by a grant funded by Widener trustee John F. Schmutz, who has expressed special interest in student engagement with community affairs. The mayor summed up the community's response, noting that "Widener students did an excellent job bringing to life . . . what Chester has to offer. This is a great example of the growth of Chester's public-private partnerships with our prestigious anchor institutions, such as Widener University."[23]

Fostering Citizenship for an Interdependent World

One of the greatest contemporary challenges is how to make our increasingly interconnected world work for the benefit of the myriad societies, cultures, and individuals who depend on its many and complex interconnections. For today's students, global connections and experiences are simply a fact of life, facilitated by the rapid expansion of new means of communication; the greater ease of travel; and the speedy circulation of images, ideas, tastes, and understandings. These have produced an interlinked but also divided and conflicted global situation, as even a casual scan of any news source reveals. The critical question, at once theoretical and practical, is how to make this uncertain interdependence work for the benefit of the world and all its inhabitants, human and nonhuman.

The key to constructively addressing this daunting challenge lies in a question that is also at once intellectually demanding and practically exigent: Can we learn to see others from different places, economic classes, social and racial groups, and other ethnicities to some serious degree as they see themselves? This is the same question that provokes the search for a civic culture in nations, societies, cities, and geographical regions. Only its full dimensions turn out to extend far beyond the immediate experience of most individuals. Grasping its proportions requires major efforts of minds and imaginations. Learning how to live constructively with a global awareness demands comparably strenuous efforts to grow in understanding difference and still poorly understood relationships. Yet these are tasks that no responsible effort at higher education for the twenty-first century can avoid. Happily, on NAC&U campuses, education for global citizenship is a common aspiration.

All NAC&U campuses offer many organized opportunities to students for learning outside the United States. Today such experiences are becoming ever more common, and not just in designated study abroad programs but throughout the curriculum. As we saw in the previous chapter, the ways campuses such as the University of Evansville use internships and placements in business organizations to foster their students' exploration of vocational possibilities also brought students into contact with the global context of contemporary business. Working with American companies, for example, brought students into contact with the economic expansion that has been taking place in some of the world's most populous nations in Asia and Latin America.

Students involved in such programs that are linked to contemporary business and its practices cannot help but learn how much U.S. firms are intertwined with suppliers elsewhere. These students sometimes travel to those societies as part of their academic courses or as interns where they also learn that these relationships of trade and investment can be competitive as well as cooperative, with American employees sometimes directly competing with peers in distant places. At the same time, some of these placements connect students with projects in those nations to enhance the skills and living situations of workers abroad or bring them into contact with the vast movements of immigrants everywhere in the world. So the students discover that globalization is complex and describes sometimes contradictory and conflictual processes, and it raises unavoidable ethical as well as economic questions.

As we saw with North Central College's immersion experiences, many students find their encounters with people and situations that are radically unlike their own environments to be moments of personal, moral, and often intellectual awakening. The impact of encountering people who lead very different lives, with different family backgrounds and expectations about their future, is often unsettling. But when properly guided, this experience also opens gateways to growth and deepened understanding. Experience abroad can underscore the complexity, exhilaration, and also the confusion of living in today's global context, often more vividly than a more typical, distanced investigation. Therefore, an important task of contemporary colleges and universities has to be preparing their students to be able to flourish and find a responsible place in such an environment. This mission is sometimes called *global education* or *educating for global citizenship.*

Global Studies at Arcadia University

The spacious lawns of Arcadia University's campus in Glenside, Pennsylvania, a suburb of Philadelphia, do not immediately reveal its identity as the nerve center of one of the nation's most ambitious efforts at global civic education. However, Arcadia's mission statement is explicit: "prepare students for lives of informed contribution in a rapidly changing global society." Arcadia sees itself as having been at the forefront of educating its students for global connection and responsibility since its predecessor, Beaver College, sponsored a study trip by a group of undergraduate women in 1948 to assist in reconstructing war-devastated Europe. Today, the university boasts a College of Global Studies. As dean of the college and university vice president, Lorna Stern said the college promises to give students "a distinctively global, integrative, and personal learning experience that prepares them to contribute and prosper in a diverse and dynamic world." The university is committed to providing rich experiences of civic engagement for its students in the Philadelphia region and in many parts of the world.

To make good on its promise, Arcadia maintains cooperative relationships with other academic institutions worldwide along with a host of community partner organizations. These carefully developed ties enable the university to provide its students with access to 130 different programs in Europe, Asia, and Africa. Altogether, about 3,000 undergraduates take part in Arcadia programs outside the United States each year, with many participants drawn from other colleges and universities. As with all good civic education programs, the College of Global Studies is not an add-on to the university's curriculum. On the contrary, its activities and offerings are deeply embedded in the courses of study. Arcadia encourages its students to integrate an international dimension into their learning in a variety of disciplines and fields. For example, students majoring in the health sciences as well as majors in the science, technology, engineering, and mathematics departments; education majors; and students in the College of Business can move easily between required courses at the main campus and locations overseas.

Arcadia aims to do more than enable students to spend time enjoying the amenities of foreign capitals or, what some students have criticized, to provide tourism that does not offer students the opportunity to meet with and learn about the lives and situations of the people who live in the places they are studying. Arcadia's aim is *civic engagement abroad.* This takes a number of forms. For example, students in political science and the social sciences with an interest in democratic governance can spend a semester as parliamentary interns, working for legislators while taking supervised course work in foreign capitals such as London, Edinburgh, Dublin, and Canberra. In these internships, students watch democracy in action in a new cultural context. By actively supporting the work of governance through their internships, students gain direct experience about how governments work in different societies around the world, which is then reflected on and analyzed in course work designed to enhance their skills in communication and critical analysis.

A number of courses offered at various global sites are designated as service-learning. Open to all students in any academic program at Arcadia, they offer critical analysis and reflection on local community-based activities such as the semester-long course in community development in Cape Town, South Africa. As Remy Bessolo posted in her blog:

> Arcadia has given us a multitude of opportunities to immerse ourselves in the culture and life of Cape Town. . . . So that, while many people see Cape Town as a bustling and growing city . . . [after a while it becomes clear that] the past still haunts the entire population.

Remy and her classmates visited Robben Island, the notorious Apartheid-era prison where Nelson Mandela spent nearly two decades as an inmate. She noted, "I could feel the people's wish to move forward but at the same time recognize and honor those who were put through unimaginable struggle." She went on to describe the poignancy of learning that their guide on Robben Island had himself been a political prisoner there. Part of what Remy and her fellow participants learned that semester was the emotional weight of the past and the moral complexity of the present in South Africa. "While it is fun to wander around the tourist areas, there are people only 30 minutes away who cannot feed themselves," she wrote. "Arcadia has given us a chance to see past the tourist destinations and jump into the culture of South Africa wholeheartedly and deeply."

Alison LaLond Wyant, assistant dean in the College of Global Studies, emphasizes that discoveries and reflections such as those in Remy's blog "reflect the exuberance of our larger body of students." The program is designed to provide experience, which can often be surprising and unscripted, and space to analyze and reflect on that experience with the help of faculty from the university and its overseas partners. As in many well-designed experiential learning settings, the encounters, discussions, and individual and group reflection can lead to major leaps in learning and sometimes marked advances in self-awareness and maturity as well. "Without prompting, many of our student bloggers write about the precise types of outcomes that we seek," Wyant said. Few outcomes could be more gratifying for an educator.

Besides the service-learning courses, Arcadia also offers experiences abroad that are explicitly intended to introduce students to social movements in a host community. At the Arcadia program in Rome, for instance, one such course gives students who are guided by knowledgeable local faculty the chance to meet and interact with groups trying to combat several of the largest social problems facing modern Italy (and not just Italy). Students study and come to understand how Italy's so-called informal or illegal economy functions. They also learn how it affects the larger society, increasing the problems of tax evasion and governmental corruption, and are introduced to the problem of organized crime and the threat it poses to Italian democratic government in the context of a European and global problem. These "social-change-focused" courses provide a firsthand way for students concerned with such issues to gain in-depth understanding and research and analysis skills that can be of major value for their future studies and careers.

Arcadia is unusual because it promotes cocurricular opportunities for civic engagement abroad. Students in any major may elect to pursue a cocurricular learning certificate, which requires 15 or more hours of work in their host community and a written project demonstrating their learning from that experience. This program is popular with students studying abroad and can be a valuable credential for those interested in working for nonprofit organizations. For example, at the Arcadia program in Athens, students volunteer at an international preschool that serves mostly the children of immigrants who have come to Greece from countries in the eastern Mediterranean, Middle East, and North Africa. As they develop a deeper understanding of the problems of refugees and the causes of contemporary migration, students return to Arcadia with lessons learned and concerns enabling them to see similar issues that face American society in a worldwide context.[24]

Conclusion: The Relevance of Civic Engagement for College

As illustrated in the programs at Arcadia University, cross-pollination between experiences abroad and deeper engagement in their learning and career goals at home is all about motivating students to search for connections among the things they are learning, which embodies the premise of civic education. Just as civic life is about finding and making connections among disparate parties for the sake of a larger benefit to all, educating for civic engagement in college seeks to instill in students a similar process of discovery of connections that can help shape the kind of people they seek to become. Engagement with civic issues, both at home and in distant settings, poses arresting challenges for learning. Students' response to such challenges can change, expand, and enrich not only their intellects but also their lives as whole people.

Educating for civic engagement on NAC&U campuses is a work in progress, as it is everywhere in higher education. But as the cases profiled in this chapter have shown, it represents an integral and important part of the mission of these institutions and offers students important opportunities for discovery and growth. This aspect of an NAC&U education ties together the other two in important ways. By focusing on the dimension of relatedness and interdependence among people and societies as well as between ideas and skills, civic engagement embodies integrated learning in very concrete ways. As we have seen, through civic participation that is carefully analyzed and reflected upon, it is possible to learn how to relate career aspirations to a widening grasp of the world. One result is a deepened sense of self-worth and possibility, a growth in the resilience that makes it possible to flourish even in an uncertain future. Another is a practical realization of what citizenship in a community, nation, and world entails: the responsibility it demands but also the sense of community, meaning, and purpose it confers.

Notes

1. A large amount of literature exists on this civic or public dimension of higher education, for example, Murchland, *Higher Education and the Practice of Democratic Politics*; Saltmarsh & Harley, *To Serve a Larger Purpose*.

2. Clydesdale, *The Purposeful Graduate*, pp. 61–65, pp. 199–204.

3. D. A. Pellegrino, personal communication, April 21, 2015.

4. Boyer, "Creating the New American College."

5. Delbanco, *College*, p. 148.

6. Roels, "An Education for Life Abundant."

7. For an analysis of the practices and effects of student participation in NetVUE and related programming, see Clydesdale, *The Purposeful Graduate*, pp. 85–129.

8. Tocqueville, *Democracy in America*, p. 506.

9. Ibid., p. 508.

10. Tocqueville, *Democracy in America*.

11. Ibid., pp. 525–528.

12. Ibid., p. 513.

13. Ibid., p. 510.

14. Ibid.

15. Ibid., pp. 525–528.

16. Ibid., p. 506.

17. Colby, Ehrlich, Beaumont, & Stephens., *Educating Citizens*, pp. 116–122.

18. North Central University, personal communication, May 2, 2015.

19. Ibid.

20. Colby et al., p. 85.

21. Ibid.

22. Ibid., pp. 213, 284ff.

23. Widener University Public Affairs Office, personal communication, February 9, 2015.

24. A. LaLond Wyant & L. Stern, personal communication, April 21, 2015.

5

AFTER THE BACHELOR'S DEGREE

Graduate Programs and Civic Professionalism

The distinctive feature of an NAC&U education, the integration of the liberal arts, professional studies, and civic engagement, does not end with the bachelor's degree. All the campuses described in the previous chapters offer graduate programs in addition to their undergraduate degrees. These programs are typically, although not entirely, in professional fields and provide students with the opportunity to earn master's degrees and, in some instances, doctorates.

Innovative Graduate Degree Programs at Pacific Lutheran University

At Pacific Lutheran University (PLU), the graduate programs incorporate strong experiential components so that graduates are better prepared to enter their chosen fields of practice. The university has a strong commitment to diversity among graduate students, and once again civic engagement plays a conspicuous role.

The marriage and family therapy master of arts program runs the Couple and Family Therapy Center, a low-cost clinic for the Parkland community near the university. The clinic offers graduate students the opportunity to gain experience as therapists while also serving a need in this underserved area of the city. The emphasis at the clinic is on experiential learning and a commitment to serving community needs. The clinic contains observation rooms and recording equipment so that students can carefully improve their skills and also gain valuable insight and feedback from their peers and faculty supervisors. The clinic experience is in addition to guaranteed internship placements at one of five off-site community mental health agencies. The program is designed to challenge students by expanding their exposure to diverse populations through both class assignments and volunteer work in the community.

According to April Knight, a second-year student in the master's program,

> I was raised to see all people as equal and that the way to show respect for others is to focus on the ways we are alike and to downplay differences. My professor challenged us to move from being color blind (ignoring racial differences) to being color brave (asking questions and seeking to understand the differences in others' experience as well as the similarities). This was a powerful paradigm shift for me. I have applied this principle, not only in regard to race, but to all differences, and have experienced the richness that comes from this approach to living. So, I have expanded the term from *color brave* to *culture brave*. Anytime I engage with someone who has a different experience than me, I now focus on being brave instead of blind, and it has made all the difference.

The innovative features of PLU's graduate curriculum are by no means confined to the marriage and family therapy program. The new master of science in marketing research program is the first program of its kind on the West Coast. Marketing research professionals provide analytical insight and inform decisions to achieve the goals of profit and nonprofit organizations. This program prepares students for one of the cutting-edge areas of contemporary business. In a fast-paced, 10-month, full-time program students study to become marketing research analysts; advertising, promotions, or marketing managers; big data analysts; or public relations specialists, for example. The program also advances students toward doctoral studies.

As in the other graduate programs in the School of Business, this one features a fast-track admission option that allows graduating students and alumni who graduated within the past five years to bypass the GRE/GMAT requirement. PLU also offers preferential admissions treatment to its graduating seniors and alumni, including a 10% discount on tuition in any of its master's degree programs.

For those who wish to explore their potential as creative writers, PLU offers a master of fine arts in creative writing, an innovative three-year residency program in poetry, fiction, and creative nonfiction. Students spend a full year with a faculty mentor, an arrangement that has proven successful for busy professionals and those who wish to take time to develop their fullest potential as writers. Combining rigor and support, each mentorship year is tailored to the participant's goals.

The program includes the Rainier Writing Workshop, held each summer on campus, which allows each participant to design an independent project to enhance his or her skills and advance specific writing goals. The workshop is directed by Rick Barot, a PLU faculty member and well-published poet who also serves as poetry editor of the *New England Review*. "It's like a mash up of a boot camp and a summer camp," Barot quipped. "It's fun but it's incredibly rigorous." Graduate students spend an intensive week with a faculty mentor and together attend workshops on their writing, talks, readings, and participate in informal conversations. This allows students to begin to develop a relationship with their mentor that they will continue through correspondence after the week is over.

Workshop alumni have generated a substantial record of success in publication, teaching, and other literary achievements. The poet laureate of Washington State for 2012–2014, Kathleen Flenniken, is a graduate, as are poet Kelli Russell Agodon (graduated in 2007); Jennifer Culkin (graduated in 2007), a nonfiction writer and winner of the prestigious Rona Jaffe Foundation Writer's Award; and Carrie Mesrobian, whose book *Sex and Violence* was named a Best Book of 2013 by *Publishers Weekly*.[1]

Leadership and Liberal Arts in North Central College

Ten years after graduating with a master of arts in education from North Central College in Naperville, Illinois, Brian Waterman was named High School Principal of the Year for 2014 by the West Cook Chapter of the Illinois Principals Association, a significant recognition of his outstanding achievements as an educator by his professional peers. Asked about the factors that had contributed to his success, Brian named his graduate education at North Central, singling out the program's emphasis on leadership development. "North Central's graduate program teaches you how to be a good leader, which applies to any industry," he said. "The program allows you to reflect on leadership principles and your leadership style."

Like most NAC&U institutions, North Central offers an array of graduate degree programs in education; business; liberal studies; Web and Internet applications; leadership studies; and specializations in sports, social entrepreneurship, and professional leadership. All graduate students are required to take one course outside their degree program. Students in education may choose to enroll in a basic marketing course, or business administration students may take a course such as Race, Ethnicity, and the American Experience in liberal studies. Because students are not restricted to choosing the elective class from a prescribed list, they can tailor a learning experience that meets their career goals as well as their personal interests. In this way, North

Central demonstrates the value of the liberal arts to graduate and under-graduate students regardless of their academic pursuit.

One of North Central's signature programs at the undergraduate level is its Leadership, Ethics, and Values program, which continues at the graduate level with a focus on leadership in many programs, such as the education cur-riculum that Brian Waterman enrolled in. It furthers the integration of civic engagement with professional preparation along with the liberal arts to foster development of involved citizens and leaders. Many of the graduate faculty also teach in the undergraduate program, and they bring to their teaching an emphasis on personal connection and engagement with their students' progress that characterizes good undergraduate teaching.

Besides leadership, North Central's graduate programs embrace the importance of teamwork as a professional skill. Most courses include a teamwork component. To further enhance the mind- and career-expanding aspects of students' graduate experience, in every program students take at least one course in which they work with others pursuing very different careers. A future principal working with a future financial analyst, both working with a high school English teacher and a retired engineer, provide an educational synergy that enhances students' ability to solve complex, real-world problems by cultivating an appreciation for the strengths of various disciplinary perspectives. It is worth noting that these features of North Central's programs are teaching at an advanced graduate level a key skill employers have identified as making applicants valuable and attrac-tive to them: the capacity to work effectively in teams with diverse other professionals.

Undergraduates interested in continuing on to graduate study at North Central can enroll in the Integrated Program, in which students earn gradu-ate credit while completing their undergraduate degree. Students can fulfill the requirements of both degrees faster, thereby helping reduce their time to degree while also reducing the cost of their education.[2]

Distinctive Features of an NAC&U Graduate Degree

These graduate programs share several important features. All NAC&U institutions offer graduate study, and some, such as PLU and North Cen-tral, offer accelerated or combined bachelor's and master's degree programs. Students who have already matriculated at an institution have the oppor-tunity to proceed directly from the bachelor's to the master's level without having the time or the expense of a separate application process. Besides the advantages of these accelerated programs, some campuses also offer special opportunities to graduates of other NAC&U institutions. All provide an array of graduate degree study opportunities whether or not they are from an NAC&U institution.[3]

This chapter introduces several more examples of the variety of NAC&U graduate programs, which are illustrative but far from exhaustive of the range of programs available. Because NAC&U institutions specialize in graduate programs oriented toward preparing students to practice in a specific profession or field, a number of the features of the NAC&U undergraduate experience also set these graduate programs apart. These programs typically have been developed in response to students' needs and demands for advanced training in certain fields. On one end, programs have been tailored to connect with the integrative undergraduate experience of the particular campus, and on the other end, programs also connect with the needs of students who are often working and busy with family life. The deep involvement of the NAC&Us in their geographic regions provides strong links to employers and networks of alumni, both of which are important to students' career success.

These features have produced highly distinctive graduate programs in NAC&U institutions that not only provide their students with excellent employment prospects in their chosen fields but also enable them to hone those distinctive skills of integrated learning that are defining features of NAC&U undergraduate programs.[4] For many graduate students who are returning to study after a period in the working world, the experience of sharing the intimate atmosphere of a campus focused on learning and connecting students to the larger world proves inspiring and an important motivation toward advancing in their careers.

Graduate Programs That Prepare Students for Good Work

Most people do not want just a job; they want good, rewarding work. They seek work that will enable them to build a career that provides not only a livelihood but also the opportunity to grow skills, increase compensation, and enhance self-respect, all elements of good work. But good work also means doing things that have serious meaning, are acknowledged as valuable by others, and are interesting and important to the individual. Developing one's abilities to engage in this kind of work is one of the most important goals of college education. It is certainly the primary goal of most students who undertake graduate degree programs, and it is the underlying aim of an NAC&U graduate education.

As noted in Chapter 3, a Gallup survey found that life satisfaction is most strongly influenced by the presence or absence of a strong attachment to a worthwhile purpose.[5] Other things are important such as strong human bonds, economic security, safety, pride in one's community, and good health;

however, the sense of engagement with meaningful work that enables a person to fulfill his or her goals is the most important of all. Without such good work it is more difficult to feel that life is worth living.

One study found that along with personal interest, the key to satisfaction is an enduring engagement with a set of values that define the work of a particular profession or field of endeavor.[6] The authors of the suggestively titled *Good Work: When Excellence and Ethics Meet* found that in field after field, the most admired practitioners were those whose careers embodied love for the activity itself and its purposes. Such excellent practitioners were more motivated by doing their jobs well and advancing the goals of their profession than they were by personal achievement or reward. In fact, they and their peers most often ascribed their outstanding success to their involvement for the sake of the work itself.[7] Like outstanding artists and athletes, it turned out that what gave them so much confidence and vitality was precisely their devotion to

> good work . . . a commitment to a body of knowledge and skill both for its own sake and for the use to which it is put . . . that allows the full expression of what is best in us, activities that exhibit the highest sense of responsibility.[8]

Those who take up their work with such an attitude become committed to "preserve, refine, and elaborate that knowledge and skill." That is, they become motivated primarily by the intrinsic rewards from the work of a profession such as teaching, nursing, medicine, engineering, law, or journalism. They typically find themselves within a context of peers who likewise seek to excel in doing such good work. The authors of the study found that this corresponded to the spirit espoused by most of the organized professions. But far from mere lip service, these outstanding performers sought to employ their highly honed skills with a commitment to solving problems in the world, "to perform [their work] well for the benefit of others—to do Good Works."[9]

The qualities the Good Work Study found to be characteristic of high-performing professionals and closely related to the sense of life satisfaction that Gallup calls purpose well-being can rightly be described as professionalism, as when someone takes a properly professional attitude toward his or her work.[10] Although these qualities are necessary to anyone who enters training for a licensed profession such as pharmacy, law, accounting, nursing, or civil engineering, they are also essential to high achievement and satisfaction in a much wider range of occupations. NAC&U institutions prepare students to enter a variety of fields, including business, computer science, social work, nursing and the allied heath professions, pharmacy, law, and engineering.

All these fields of professional work depend on students who have mastered the knowledge and skill that underlie their practice but who have also committed themselves to using their work to contribute to the lives of the people they will serve. Therefore, just as professionals are said to practice their professions when they work (i.e., they bring the values of that profession to bear for the benefit of clients or patients), taking a professional attitude toward any occupation can turn that work into a practice whereby the workers aim to do genuinely good work.

If a spirit of professionalism is so valuable, even essential, for a meaningful and successful career, how is it acquired? Graduate professional education in many fields has been moving toward employing some of the same high-impact learning practices used in the best undergraduate programs. One of the most important insights offered by the learning sciences is that the most effective learning happens when students are challenged and supported in trying out their knowledge by putting it to use. For this reason, the use of cases, simulations, and actual clinical and field experience is very important. The good news is that it is becoming ever more widespread. The experience of faculty with these pedagogies at the graduate and undergraduate levels can be a real help in making graduate programs highly effective.

In addition, these more active forms of learning have particular importance in graduate professional programs because their simulation or actual involvement of practice makes it more possible, and makes it feel more natural, to engage students in learning what it means to be a professional. Learning professional practice in a clinical setting enables teachers to point out to students how certain dispositions and attitudes toward the work affects patients and clients. Many students have noted how important awareness of their responsibilities toward the welfare of others has been for shaping their own sense of identity as professionals.[11] Also important, say students, is the recognition they receive in these settings of practice from mentors and peers that confirms their own developing sense of identity as professionals. Many NAC&U programs have designed forms of learning to practice that give their students contact with people and communities who can most benefit from professional services. This can greatly help students integrate a leaning toward civic engagement with active learning of the knowledge and skills that mark a genuine professional. To better understand how this spirit of professionalism is developed in NAC&U graduate professional study, here we consider a few more examples of professional programs.

Widener University's Innovative Clinics

For more than a decade, Widener University has provided an important part of the education of graduate students in nursing, physical therapy, and clinical psychology in five clinics the university operates in the nearby, economically depressed city of Chester, Pennsylvania. The nursing clinic, opened in October 2011, is the newest of the university's clinics, and its staff have treated more than 1,200 people since opening its doors. Four other Widener clinics serve the residents of Chester: the Chester Community Physical Therapy Clinic and three mental health clinics that are staffed by the Institute of Graduate Clinical Psychology, including faculty and students in the provision of care. The physical therapy clinic is run by faculty and students of the doctoral program in physical therapy.

All five clinics provide services for either medical or mental health issues at reduced rates based on the patients' ability to pay. The nursing clinic and physical therapy clinic offer free services to those who can't afford any expense. In Chester, where about one third of the city's population lives below the poverty level, Widener health care experts said these clinics were filling a great need even as the national Affordable Care Act was being implemented. "There will always be a need for such clinics," said John Culhane, a Widener law professor and director of the university's Health Law Institute. "Even if all the pieces of the Affordable Care Act fall into place, there will be a need for community-based services."

These clinics were inspired in part by the university's pioneering Social Work Counseling Services (SWCS), a program founded in 2000 to give Widener social work students experience in counseling and serving members of the community in need. Since its inception, more than 3,000 people have received counseling or participated in programs organized by SWCS, and 200 social work students have served about 4,000 people in Chester and surrounding communities. Provost Stephen Wilhite, who served as dean of the School of Human Service Professions during the inception of the SWCS and then of the clinics, said the SWCS was very influential on the newer clinics.

> It provided an example for us of how clinics could serve the community in a way that would not only benefit residents, but how we could provide experience for students in professional programs. . . . These clinics also present faculty with research opportunities and give them another way to participate in the community through the supervision of students.

With the deliberate aim of integrating the work of various professional fields into the provision of care for community members who would not otherwise have access to these important services, these clinics model civic engagement in professional work for nursing, physical therapy, and clinical psychology graduate students. For example, the physical therapy clinic has grown under the direction of the program's doctoral students to earn respect nationwide. A total of 174 patients visited the clinic 2,435 times in its first four years of operation. Through donations and hard work by the students, the campus space housing the clinic was stocked with exercise equipment and now compares favorably with professional physical therapy facilities. All students in the doctoral program have volunteered in the clinic under the supervision of licensed physical therapists. "It's completely student run," said Caitlin Grobaker, a graduate student in the program. "We make our own funding, and we take care of patients. The fact that we have this clinic, and that it's part of a cycle of our program, is just amazing."

The clinic's success is influencing other universities around the country. Administrators of the doctoral program launched a national network of pro bono clinics, a national pro bono physical therapy honor society, and plans to host student-run seminars over the Internet. Scott Voshell, a 2008 alumnus of the Widener program who is now a practicing physical therapist, said he has witnessed the success of the clinic as chair of the American Physical Therapy Association's Global Health Special Interest Group. "I am privy to watching the growth of student-run physical therapy pro bono clinics," he said, "and Widener is leading the way."

Volunteers and donations also help to run the nursing clinic, said Ellen Boyda, coordinator of the family nurse practitioner program for the School of Nursing, who founded and directs the nursing clinic. Most of the equipment and medicines in the three treatment rooms at the nursing clinic came from donations. The biggest need now is for nurse practitioner volunteers, Boyda said. "I truly believe there will always be a need for clinics like this one—there are people who fall through the cracks," she said. "The need is more than we can handle, but we are doing something nevertheless." This can-do spirit is one of the contagious effects of using the clinic as part of students' clinical education. It is another instance of how learning to use professional knowledge in contexts of great patient need helps students bring together their technical expertise with their ethical understandings, which are key ingredients in a career trajectory aimed toward good work.[12]

Widener's Unique Doctoral Program in Nursing

The School of Nursing has also developed a unique doctoral program focused on "the science of nursing education." In 2013 the Widener University School of Nursing was selected as a Center of Excellence for its doctoral program, which is specifically directed at educating future nurse educators and researchers who want to advance the science of nursing education. The program provides students with experience in pedagogical research and evidence-based teaching practice. It also aims to disseminate its findings within and beyond the School of Nursing to outside nurse educators and scholars. The program emphasizes role modeling and coaching of faculty, encouraging faculty to explore innovative teaching practices and technology as well as engaging the students in the learning process. Although many doctoral programs in nursing focus on clinical practice, very few share Widener's emphasis on contributing to the field of nursing education. Graduates of the program have begun to have significant influence nationally and internationally on developments in the field of nursing education.[13]

Graduate Learning in Science, Technology, Engineering, and Mathematics

In today's highly technological environment, science, technology, engineering, and mathematics (STEM) enjoy a high profile. As noted in earlier chapters, NAC&U campuses provide a wide variety of undergraduate programs attuned to current student demand and the needs of the growing research and technology industries. At the graduate level too, the member schools of the consortium offer a significant range of programs for the master's and doctorate degrees that seek to appeal to students who want the best preparation for future professional work while also continuing to expand their understanding of the larger world and deepen their sense of civic commitment. Like others we have explored, these STEM programs are focused on preparing future professionals to do good work.

Engineering at Manhattan College

At Manhattan College, the School of Engineering offers degrees in chemical, civil, computer, electrical, and mechanical engineering. As students prepare to enter the profession of engineering or associated occupations, they are guided toward future careers by three values. They are expected to "know and embrace *ethical behavior*, participate in the larger *community,* and show a commitment to *service* to humankind and the environment." These three pillars of the college's undergraduate curriculum deliberately extend into graduate programs. Emanating from the college's Catholic and Lasallian heritage, these values are reinforced in the tone and teaching of the curriculum at the undergraduate level and into the graduate level. Administrators of the engineering school see it as a strong professional school in a liberal arts college.

Examples of the close linkage between the professional preparation offered to master's students and the college's concern with service to humankind and the environment are its master of science and master of engineering degrees in environmental engineering. The program is one of only four such accredited programs in the United States and enjoys a worldwide reputation for pioneering work in this emerging field. The school is also linked directly with the larger New York metropolitan construction community through the construction management option in the civil engineering program.

This option is extremely popular because many of the school's graduates enter the construction field, giving them access to careers as engineers. Recent graduate Victoria Scala remarked, "I have seen the civil engineering program full circle. Being in New York City, professors can use projects they are currently working on as examples for their students, thus bringing a true real-world example to the classroom." Now teaching part-time as an adjunct professor, Scala can underscore from her own path how this linking of theory to experience "helps the students to be successful in advancing their careers."

As with a number of other programs at NAC&Us, Manhattan College's engineering school is designed to enable professionals already in the workplace to achieve advanced degrees. It also offers a five-year, seamless master's program, which enables a qualified undergraduate student to begin taking engineering courses for graduate credit. Thus, while still an undergraduate, a Manhattan College student can complete up to nine credit hours that can be applied toward requirements for the master's degree. The remaining credit hours can be completed with one additional year of study, for a total of five years from the beginning of college.

According to Maureen Hayes,

> Upon completing my [undergraduate] degree in chemical engineering, I wasn't sure what I wanted to go into, but the seamless master's program enabled me to explore multiple career options and further develop my skills in chemical engineering and to enter the business world as a young adult. . . . Aside from the technical aspects required for a master's degree in chemical engineering, the program gave [me] the opportunity to develop my leadership skills, time management, strategic thinking, and problem solving in an environment where professors are always willing and eager to answer questions and discuss new ideas and provide guidance on the students' journeys.

Her openness to the exploration of career possibilities was clearly, in her estimation, made possible by curricular structure but actively supported by the interest and concern of her faculty. This enabled her to employ the values of liberal learning she had acquired as an undergraduate to open up her range of possibilities for making a successful transition to the world of work.

One of the noteworthy aspects of Manhattan's graduate engineering program is an international connection. To foster a broader perspective and civic engagement in the global environment, students may also work toward their master's degree at a sister institution in France, making it possible for them to graduate with a dual engineering degree valid in the United States and France. This program enables graduate students to experience the global nature and contribution of the STEM fields as well as pursue careers with international dimensions. Here, too, students encounter the values of liberal learning and civic engagement as integral aspects of their preparation as engineering professionals.

Manhattan's programs are part of a group of NAC&U campuses with strong engineering programs. Belmont University, Hampton University, Ohio Northern University, PLU, University of Evansville, University of Scranton, Valparaiso University, and Widener University are the other members of this set of consortium members, each with its own unique mix of degree programs and options for engineering study.[14]

Pharmacy at Ohio Northern University

Ohio Northern University is the mainstay institution of the small town of Ada, located in Harden County. Its Raabe College of Pharmacy is one of the oldest such programs in Ohio, and its graduates constitute one in four of the licensed pharmacists in the state. Raabe offers only one degree program: a six-year combined bachelor of science/doctor of pharmacy curriculum that enables incoming college freshmen to graduate six years later as doctors of pharmacy. As the administrators of the school like to say, its graduates are genuinely "practice-ready."

Because Raabe's program is continuous throughout undergraduate and graduate study, students have exactly the kind of integrated program of study that is the NAC&U hallmark. While the program is clearly centered on the STEM fields that support the practice of pharmacy, it also includes a strong liberal arts core. It pulls together requirements for broad, general thinking abilities; an understanding of diverse cultures and their effects on human interaction, informed by ethical responses; and educated responses to aesthetics in art and nature. Pharmacy students are also major participants in the university's athletic and arts programs. Moreover, the liberal arts emphasis of the program is complemented by a stress on community involvement and civic engagement.

Some of these integrative features are deliberately woven into the professional program itself. Beginning in freshman year and continuing through the more specialized placements of the graduate years of the program, students experience the interdisciplinary nature of pharmacy practice by means of their rotation through a wide range of sites, from hospitals to community pharmacies to direct patient interaction in diverse settings. Pharmacy's nature as a profession that draws on several fundamental sciences while also embodying the values of care in human interaction makes it a natural setting for integrating the emphases of liberal education with scientific rigor and experiential learning.

The new Harden County multidisciplinary mobile health clinic, supported by federal funds and developed in cooperation with Harden County health agencies, provides care in often-neglected rural areas of Ohio Northern's hinterland as it becomes a new site for the licensed supervising of pharmacy students' clinical education.

"We have dynamic students who are excited about contributing to the community in positive ways and helping residents get the health care services they need, as well as gaining valuable hands-on experience," said Steven Martin at the inception of the clinic. "Because Ohio Northern University is committed to assisting the community, we worked with county health officials to establish this new resource to assist residents who might not otherwise receive the medical attention they need," he said. Something of that student dynamism toward civic engagement achieved recognition in 2015 when a fifth-year pharmacy student, Jeremiah Barnes, won a prestigious award from the U.S. Public Health Service for his involvement in community professional outreach by bringing health services to elderly residents of the community.[15]

Graduate Management Education at The Sage Colleges

The Sage Colleges of Troy and Albany are strategically placed in New York state's capital region, often now referred to as its emerging Tech Valley. Within this context, the Sage School of Management provides several graduate programs designed for working professionals who are seeking ways to advance in their careers. These programs are also targeted to specific segments of the regional economy, notably the burgeoning health care industry, state and local government, and small enterprise.

The theme throughout the School of Management is careful tailoring of advanced degree programs to fit student career needs but also connect with developments in the regional economy. Faculty members work closely with students, which, as previously noted, is a key to student motivation in every educational context. But it is especially valuable to graduate students who must balance ongoing commitments to work and family with their new learning. This emphasis has produced programs with a unique structure or content, such as the health services administration master of science degree. What might elsewhere be generic courses in accounting, finance, marketing, and management, are here focused on the specific features of the health care industry, enabling students to develop competences that will help them navigate the complexities of careers in this large and varied sector.

A signature of the school's efforts to enable its graduates to become flexible and civically attuned professionals is its culminating experience and project requirement. This is an important contribution of liberal learning to the Sage School of Management's graduate curriculum. This component of the curriculum, which is required of graduate students in the organization management and business administration programs as well as health services administration, helps students place their growing professional expertise in a wider perspective that marks effective leadership and good work. As mostly working professionals, students can bring considerable and diverse experiences to these integrative efforts, enabling them to expand their perspectives on their future careers. Typically, the culminating experience is a consulting project with a local business or nonprofit, a requirement that builds a direct civic component into the programs. In the health services administration curriculum, for example, the marketing course features a hands-on project involving a nonprofit health care organization.

These aspects of the program seem clear to alumni and much valued by them. As one successful graduate of the MBA program, John Bellardini, summed up his appreciation, "Business leaders should be able to help others—to see another perspective, to make difficult decisions, and to embrace change." And that, said Bellardini, "is what Sage prepared me for. There was a touch of heart, a sensibility that you don't often get in business school about understanding people." This has served Bellardini well. He is now vice president for finance at Chobani Foods.

The school of management enables undergraduates enrolled in Russell Sage College and Sage College of Albany to apply for graduate study through a shortened application process and receive a discount on tuition. In addition, incoming students can elect to proceed toward their master's degree directly in a 4 + 1 accelerated program to obtain the degree within five years of beginning college.[16]

Integrating the Arts in Westminster College's Graduate Studies

At Westminster College in Salt Lake City, Utah, the graduate programs have benefited from the college's reorganization of its undergraduate curriculum to foster more integration between the liberal arts and professional studies. Westminster's deepening appreciation of the value of the liberal arts for connecting and deepening students' professional learning in the graduate programs has had an impact on the campus. The liberal arts also play significant roles in the curricula of other schools, including the master of business program.

For example, in the School of Nursing and the Health Sciences, students working on master's degrees now routinely receive assignments that emphasize a more focused reading of texts, complemented with reflective writing exercises to assist students in applying the perspectives derived from readings in the humanities and social sciences to the practice of nursing and the health sciences.

In the School of Education, graduate students also receive targeted practice in critical thinking, reinforced by reflective writing exercises. Instead of simply being presented with various philosophies of education, students are challenged to examine them, comparing and contrasting approaches and the differing implications for teaching practice. Such pedagogical techniques derived from the arts and sciences are also used to help education students become more reflective about their own practice. These features of the curriculum are particularly appropriate for a school that seeks to make social justice and the improvement of education its defining values.

Student response to the inclusion of liberal learning approaches in graduate programs has been positive. For example, an MBA graduate commented,

> The MBA program emphasized team projects and group work, allowing for leadership and teamwork opportunities that helped me in my career; the writing and communication skills I learned at Westminster allow me to empower people to be responsible and own their results.

Another said,

> Westminster taught me critical, analytical, and integrative thinking by requiring me to track, reevaluate, and adjust every decision I made. I've seen that these are the abilities that set me apart from other people who might aspire to work in the same field I'm in.

The integrative impulse is perhaps most evident in Westminster College's master's program in community leadership offered in the School of Education. Like several other NAC&U institutions, Westminster places considerable emphasis on developing leadership among its students at the undergraduate and graduate levels. But it is unusual to offer a program that enables nonprofit and community leaders to continue to hone their skills in organizational management, research, marketing, and more, and receive a credential for doing so.

Along with this high-profile role of the liberal arts in its graduate programs, Westminster also emphasizes the value of civic engagement in preparing for professional careers. All the graduate programs have civic platforms and events. For instance, students in nursing and the health fields provide information and testimony at the state legislature regarding health care bills, participate in community service health care projects such as basic health assessment activities in low-income and senior health clinics, and provide community support for venues and events in the community where public health has to be monitored. Education students serve in similar community-focused efforts to improve educational programs and outcomes through the college's partnership with the city of South Salt Lake.

Throughout its graduate programs, Westminster College is attempting to further the NAC&U hallmark of integrated learning by extending it to preparing students for careers that will have impact on the educational, business, health care, and civic sectors of the greater Salt Lake metropolis.[17]

Graduate Preparation in an Integrated and Civic Spirit

Higher education faces the challenge of preparing students to thrive amid the continuing churn of the American economy. The mass media provide a nearly continuous stream of information about rapid and often unsettling changes in the kinds of jobs available to today's college graduates and their prospects for future careers. Advanced degrees are becoming ever more important as entry tickets for admission to the best of these career paths, but graduates find that even those are often subject to change without notice. This is the overwhelming fact that makes deciding on a college major and then a graduate program difficult and sometimes risky.

In the face of these uncertainties, institutions of higher learning more than ever must develop educational experiences to enable students to cope with the challenges they will face after graduation. An NAC&U education provides a strong platform for students to build their futures because it integrates professional preparation with liberal learning and experience with civic engagement. Administrators at these campuses are committed to achieving in practice what Andrew Delbanco said is "at the core of the college idea . . . that to serve others is to serve oneself by providing a sense of purpose, thereby countering the loneliness and aimlessness by which all people, young and old, can be afflicted."[18]

The centerpiece of this strategy is the focus on student learning as the holistic outcome of the entire organization of the campus, its staff, and its educational activities. As we have seen through many examples, this focus guides efforts to include practical experience, reflection, and engagement in the world through intellectual training and exploration. As we have seen in this chapter, this holistic emphasis provides a distinctive environment for graduate study. Because they are necessarily specialized to provide advanced training, graduate programs focus intensively on educating students in the knowledge, skills, and dispositions proper to a particular domain. But there is also a common aim: to develop students' qualities of mind and spirit that will enable them to succeed in doing good work over a career that may take them into many different areas of practice.

These habits of mind are "generic" thinking skills, or "underlying analytical competencies." These capacities are the means by which the values of intellectual cultivation meet the economic realities of today's job market. These abilities, deeply embedded in liberal education, have outpaced all others to emerge as the key to higher-paying jobs and more successful careers in today's highly competitive "information economy."[19]

The Payoff of Integrated Learning in Today's Economy

The evidence for the preeminent value of these thinking skills is very strong. Large-scale surveys of employers conducted over several years by the American Association of Colleges & Universities as well as a major study undertaken by the College Board found that the ability to inquire about and analyze information, synthesize knowledge, think creatively, communicate well in writing and in speech, and other similar broad capacities are the most sought after traits by employers in their hiring.[20] Even more striking is the rise in the economic value of the financial return on these skills over the long term. In summarizing this trend, sociologists Arum and Roska said that "the defining feature . . . of the last thirty years has been a precipitous increase in the wage payoff to jobs requiring synthesis, critical thinking, and inductive and deductive reasoning."[21]

The instability of the contemporary labor market has helped make these generic or underlying intellectual competencies, which are the core of liberal learning, so important to career success. People who have these skills can understand and navigate complexity. The skills are also essential for making effective judgments in uncertain situations, and they are the foundation of insight and deep understanding. Since these are precisely the qualities needed for good professional work, the value of integrating liberal learning into professional preparation is obvious and strong. And this understanding has guided the increasing incorporation of the practices and the spirit of liberal learning into graduate degree programs.

The Fit of Integrated Learning With the Resilience Agenda

The uncertainties of the current job market along with the greater flexibility demanded by today's more complex pattern of personal and family relationships have also made the quality of resilience, or grit, so important for students and graduates alike. Developing resilience is closely tied to finding long-term purposes for living. Much research has demonstrated this connection.[22] Finding purpose, we have also noted, is facilitated by a campus culture that promotes serious exploration of future career possibilities while it supports students' growth in the previously mentioned intellectual capacities that enable them to make sense of the larger world and interact in it.[23]

The process that underlies these developments is the quest for self-knowledge that has long been the heart of liberal arts education. The historical source of this conception of education is often traced to Socrates, the ancient Greek philosopher who famously declared that "the unexamined life is not worth living."[24] As students of the liberal arts know, for Socrates the examined life went beyond discovering one's competitive advantages and how to maximize them. While those abilities are undoubtedly necessary to thrive in today's highly competitive world, they do not resolve the question Socrates kept insisting was even more important: What is worth doing with one's capacities, what is worth living for? [25]

If part of the answer to the Socratic question is to be able to do good work, then students inevitably find themselves drawn into connections with others who share this quest and, especially in graduate programs, with those who share an aspiration to succeed in a profession or an occupation. In the social context of campus life, and especially in graduate programs focused on acquiring the skills of a particular field, students can grow as people. They are recognized as having a contribution to make, and as we have heard graduate students say, they expand their sense of what they can do, who they are, and for whom they are responsible. They discover that their own identity is at stake in their learning. This imports a seriousness to their lives as student professionals.

These students become more resilient because they are developing what psychologist William Damon calls life purposes, which provide a deep motivation to acquire values that guide the many individual particular decisions of life toward weaving a larger pattern. Life purposes provide motivation to "accomplish something that is at the same time meaningful to the self and consequential for the world beyond the self."[26] Individuals who succeed in discovering such purposes find they have the motivation to keep going in the face of life's inevitable but potentially discouraging setbacks and adversities.

Self-Interest Rightly Understood as the Spirit of Professionalism

We might say, then, that grounding one's growth in a worthwhile life purpose, the Socratic goal of liberal learning, describes an educational agenda that promotes resilience. The integration of the exploratory practices of liberal learning with the competence- and confidence-building features of professional study is its necessary condition. And the discovery of life purpose, which provides the key motivation for intellectual and personal growth, is sufficient condition for fostering resilience. But discovering and achieving such purposes that are meaningful to the individual but also significant for others are the real goal. They make graduate education, like the college experience, worthwhile. The quest for purpose achieved has another inherent aspect: It develops a particular sense of personal identity akin to what we saw earlier as the spirit of professionalism.

This educational agenda resonates with what Chapter 4 introduced as the *civic culture on campus*, what Alexis de Tocqueville identified in *Democracy in America* as the logic of democratic civic culture. Tocqueville called it the use of "self-interest rightly understood" to counterbalance the potentially anarchic effects of the pursuit of individual self-interest.[27] Although American society has long celebrated the individual entrepreneur, it has also been able to contain and channel those energies to attempt to achieve social justice and strengthen social bonds.

According to Tocqueville, the logic of American public institutions worked to bring individualistic Americans into associations (we might note the American penchant to form teams and clubs in business as well as in sports and the arts) that imposed a tight discipline on their members.[28] Such voluntary, collective discipline enabled large numbers of people who began as strangers to forge bonds of trust and cooperation in pursuit of a common purpose. They came to understand that their own self-interest was best served by trading anarchic impulses for sustained commitment because such cooperation enhanced their own possibilities and expanded their sense of dignity and self-worth. They recognized themselves, and were seen by their peers, as contributing members of the larger life of a democratic society.[29] Civic culture expanded individuals' imaginations. It was an alchemy that transmuted self-regarding individuals into citizens able to advance the common good and sustain free and fair institutions.

Nowhere is this logic of what Tocqueville called "self-interest rightly understood" better illustrated than in professions.[30] In occupations such as accounting, law, nursing, medicine, teaching, pharmacy, or civil engineering, individuals gain their credibility with the public only through certification by the licensing body of that profession. Behind these legal requirements, a logic similar to that of self-interest rightly understood is at work. Professional licensing benefits the public as a whole. But the individual clients, patients, and practitioners themselves also benefit. For the practitioners, their licenses serve literally as credentials, proof that their claim to expertise and responsibility can be trusted, which is why they often are posted on the walls of the doctor's or lawyer's office.

So, the public regulation of some professional occupations promotes the common good. The self-interest of all parties is protected: Patients and clients can trust that they will benefit and not be harmed or financially exploited, and the practitioner also benefits from the acceptance that public accreditation provides. From cooperating with the general rules, each receives benefits they would have to expend a great deal of energy and resources trying to obtain otherwise, as many learn the hard way from dealings with unlicensed service providers.

Toward Civic Professionalism

Modern society depends on the integrity of the impersonal structures of law, economy, and government, as the financial crisis of 2008 and its aftermath revealed all too clearly. The paradox is that although the reliability of these institutions enables individuals to pursue their particular goals, the institutions themselves can be sustained only by citizens who see their self-interest aligned with maintaining the integrity of these institutions, even at some cost to their immediate, personal self-interest.

Because it creates the climate in which such institutional integrity can be sustained, a professional spirit in an occupation, an organization, or an individual practitioner, then, is a public resource. It is a good all can share but depends heavily on the effort and goodwill of those who provide the service or product. In professional life, in business, in any sector of a complex society, establishing and maintaining a professional spirit is a demanding task. Especially when organizations are unstable and contracts of short duration, individuals feel threatened and their immediate advantage can crowd out all other considerations.

At such times, sustaining professional values, ultimately enhancing life satisfaction as well as making the larger society function better for all individuals, requires innovative thinking. It also requires leadership, skill, and stamina to persuade wavering others to follow a positive course. Students who graduate from today's graduate programs will inevitably face these issues. They will feel strong pressure to pad their résumé, to appear to be competent over making an effort at actual improvement, to be a winner at nearly any cost. Preparing students to understand and deal constructively with these situations will show the worth of graduate programs attuned to the civic spirit of professionalism.[31]

To think professionally at such moments, to take leadership among one's peers, requires just the skills and abilities this chapter emphasizes in reviewing NAC&U graduate programs. The intellectual skills imparted by liberal learning—to grasp the multiple features of a problem, to do justice to the points of view of various stakeholders in a decision situation, to communicate clearly and effectively in moments of deliberation—make it possible to escape being overwhelmed by complexity. These skills underwrite the technical expertise acquired in advanced degree programs by helping guide its application. Clinical placements are forms of learning that ground these perspectives in experience. By bringing all these dimensions together, such programs offer students an educational milieu that fosters the resilience that can make the difference between success and failure.

By pointing their students toward a professional spirit that acknowledges the human and social context of their future careers, such graduate programs make a public contribution. If we are to name the mission of this education in the NAC&U context of integrated learning, it is to prepare civic professionals.

Notes

1. Pacific Lutheran University, personal communication, August 17, 2015.
2. Northern Central University, personal communication, July 23, 2015.
3. N. Hensel, personal communication, July 15, 2015.
4. Association of American Colleges and Universities, *An Introduction to LEAP*.
5. Gallup & Purdue University, *Great Jobs Great Lives*.
6. Gardner, Csikszentmihalyi, & Damon, *Good Work*.
7. Ibid.
8. Ibid., p. 7.
9. Ibid., p. 210.
10. Gallup & Purdue University, *Great Jobs Great Lives*, pp. 3, 7.
11. For example, a national study of nursing students by the Carnegie Foundation for the Advancement of Teaching found this experience of responsibility to be crucial in their own sense of having "become" a nurse; see Benner, Sutphen, Leonard, & Day, *Educating Nurses*, pp. 21–22.
12. S. Starnes, personal communication, August 18, 2015.
13. School of Nursing, Widener University, personal communication, August 18, 2015.
14. School of Engineering, Manhattan College, personal communication August 18, 2015.
15. College of Pharmacy, Ohio Northern University, personal communication, July 3, 2015.
16. K. Fredericks, personal communication, July 2, 2015.
17. Public Affairs Office, Westminster College, personal communication, July 2, 2015.
18. Delbanco, *College*, p. 148.
19. Arum & Roksa, *Aspiring Adults Adrift*, pp. 18–21.

20. Baum, Ma, & Payea, *Education Pays*; Association of American Colleges and Universities, *An Introduction to LEAP*.

21. Arum & Roksa, *Aspiring Adults Adrift*, p. 19.

22. Damon, *Path to Purpose*, pp. 33ff; Clydesdale, *The Purposeful Graduate*, pp. 199–207.

23. See Chapter 3 in this book as well as Clydesdale, *The Purposeful Graduate*, pp. 199–207.

24. Plato, *Apology*, 38a.

25. Ibid.

26. Damon, *Path to Purpose*, p. 33.

27. Tocqueville, *Democracy in America*, pp. 525ff.

28. Ibid., pp. 509–516.

29. Ibid.

30. Ibid.

31. I developed these themes, including their application to professional preparation, in Sullivan, *Work and Integrity*.

CONCLUSION

This book provides an introduction to the education offered by the 25 institutions that make up the NAC&U consortium and an inside perspective on the educational experience these campuses offer to their students. Along the way, it has provided lots of introductions. I hope you have been as engaged by reading these as I was in providing them.

A Short Guide to the NAC&U Educational Agenda

An educational agenda summarizes the goals and intentions that guide an institution's choice of subjects to teach and the sequence and ordering of educational activities. It also makes possible certain kinds of relationships between educators and their students, among the educators themselves, and between the campus and the larger public. Such agendas are in some cases tacit; in organizations such as NAC&U they are explicit. But either way, they guide what happens in schools and colleges, and, in the end, shape students' experiences.

The order of the chapters is intended to lead the reader through that educational agenda. At the outset, the book introduces the NAC&U founders' vision of a distinctly American style of higher education, one that strives to "integrate liberal arts, professional studies, and civic responsibility." The founders realized at the beginning that achieving that vision would depend on how well the member institutions could make the various parts of campus life work together to create a sense of what they called "wholeness." This sense of community, they stressed, was the enabling condition for the kind of education they sought to foster because it anticipated and prepared students for the challenge of making the larger democratic society work in ways that would benefit everyone and leave no one out.

Chapter 1 illustrates this most basic aspect of the NAC&U agenda by presenting a kaleidoscope of contemporary examples drawn from various campuses, emphasizing the relevance of that vision for today's students. In a time of anxiety about the value of college degrees, NAC&U's agenda of an integrated educational experience equips students with abilities that correspond to the qualities most sought after by contemporary employers, according to national surveys. These are also the capacities citizens need to be able to take an active part in democratic life in a complex and interconnected world.

Chapter 2 focuses on a series of examples of how different institutions go about this integration in their undergraduate curricula, presenting a range of programs and methods that include new student orientation, connected courses, student-faculty research, team projects, internships, service-learning, and study abroad. This chapter underscores the important fact that many of these teaching practices are based on contemporary understandings of how students learn most effectively.

Chapter 3 presents a number of case studies of how NAC&U campuses weave intellectual development with personal growth through a rich social and cultural life, including sports and the arts. A positive campus climate in turn enables students to connect their college learning with preparation for future careers. The cases presented in this chapter illustrate how different campuses integrate students into the high-quality relationships with faculty and other students that motivate students toward academic success and the fruitful exploration of future career paths. The chapter profiles a number of internship and placement programs that enable students to explore occupational interests in connection with academic study.

Chapter 4 addresses the issue of how campuses integrate civic engagement with professional study and liberal arts exploration. It presents stories of programs that use connections with the world beyond the campus to expand students' understanding by interweaving their academic learning with civic endeavors. The chapter introduces research findings that support the educational value of civic learning, showing how these principles are illustrated in NAC&U programs, including several that feature environmental concerns and international and intercultural education.

Finally, Chapter 5 shows how the themes of the NAC&U agenda extend beyond the undergraduate years into distinctive programs of graduate professional study. The chapter presents a range of such programs along with student testimony about their effectiveness in preparing graduates to bring this integrated approach into their present and future careers. The chapter summarizes a major theme of the book by presenting the formation of competent and responsible professionals whose civic orientation motivates engagement in good work as an educational goal.

The Point of This Agenda

This book provides an introduction to the NAC&U educational agenda and simultaneously extends an invitation to readers to join a key part of that agenda: to imagine college as an important part of the search for a life worth living. Since the founding of the consortium in the 1990s, through two decades of innovation and adaptation, its members have remained committed to a common overarching purpose: to enable students to know who they are and the world they inhabit while preparing them to become energetically and responsibly involved in their relationships with family and community, the economy, the nation, the world, and the natural environment.

The roots of this agenda go back to Socrates, the ancient Greek philosopher who began what has become the tradition of liberal arts education by insisting that "the unexamined life is not worth living." Examining one's life in a Socratic spirit means more than grasping one's competitive advantage in the job market and how to maximize it, although it may include such aspects of self-knowledge. But self-understanding remains superficial until a person is willing and able to confront the full human import of Socrates's persistent questioning: What is really worth doing with one's abilities? Answering that question requires taking the risk of answering for oneself the big question of what is worth living for. This is why liberal learning comes first in the NAC&U agenda: It provides the platform that unites students in their individual quests to integrate professional preparation and civic engagement.

To address these Socratic questions is to start on the path to discovering meaning and purpose. Purpose, and the deep motivation it provides, is the hidden strength of people who show grit or resilience in the face of adversity. But discovering purpose, examining one's life, is not a simple or once-and-for-all matter. The aim of college is to enable students to make this quest their own. As we have seen, this means expanding the imagination as well as honing thinking skills. And the success of this educational mission depends heavily on providing a campus where social relationships, between students and faculty and among students, enable everyone to be recognized as somebody with a contribution to make. This is a climate in which students can grow as people, opening themselves to new thoughts and new possibilities, expanding their sense of what they can do, who they are, and also for whom they need to be responsible. It is what growing up and becoming adult are really about. In this most important sense, college is the real world in concentrated form.

As they make these goals explicit and build curricula and campus life around them, NAC&U institutions can offer their students what they need from higher education. Particularly for today's student generation, whose members will inevitably confront an uncertain job market along with the complexities of a wide range of choices in personal lifestyle and relationships, NAC&U's educational agenda seems to be a good fit.

For anyone considering colleges, this book provides an opportunity to probe the NAC&U agenda as a possible path through higher education. To continue these considerations by exploring specific campuses and programs in more depth, see Appendix A.

Growing Toward the Future

This book begins with the idea that by exploring the NAC&U efforts to achieve its agenda for an integrated educational experience, we would have the outline of a model for higher education for the twenty-first century that includes the following features:

1. Courses of study that integrate the broad aims of the liberal arts, development of professional competence, and a sense of civic responsibility
2. Practices of teaching and learning that engage and promote student learning through employment of high-impact practices tested by research
3. Campus community climate characterized by inclusive yet demanding expectations shared among students and faculty that support healthy relationships and personal growth
4. Cultivation of relationships between campus and the larger community and world to support educational experiences that enhance students' professional and career developments as well as their commitment to civic partnership and service to the world

A model is not a description of the way things are in detail but an ideal that is rooted in actual educational practice. The examples presented throughout the previous chapters have documented forms of integrated education as practiced in NAC&U institutions. Without claiming universal success for these efforts, the chapters have also provided theoretical interpretations of how and why these practices, and the characteristics of the campus environments that support them, contribute to successful learning and personal development. The model seeks to draw out the larger, ideal conception the ongoing work of these NAC&U educators points to.

Projecting this model is a way to sketch a clearer picture of where the educational agenda and practical efforts of these institutions are leaning. In another sense, the function of such a model is to clarify the collective identity of these campuses by projecting what their efforts might be like if fully and exuberantly undertaken. By presenting a larger conception of their enterprise, the model may enable the educators to recognize that they and their daily activities have a larger significance. But this model also points beyond the consortium. On the one hand, I hope this book provides the participants in the enterprise, current and prospective, with a sense of the power and significance of what these academic communities are committed to achieving. On the other hand, the model is also intended as a challenge to enhance the value and effectiveness of college learning by integrating professional preparation in an approach to the liberal arts that values civic purposes and commitment.

About the New American Colleges and Universities

Founded in 1995, the New American Colleges and Universities (NAC&U) is a national consortium of selective, small to mid-size (2,000–7,500 students) independent colleges and universities dedicated to the purposeful integration of liberal education, professional studies, and civic engagement. NAC&U campuses collectively and individually are often cited as models of the intentional integration of teaching and learning, scholarship, and service.

For additional information, please visit: www.newamericancolleges.org

APPENDIX A

CAMPUS PROFILES

Arcadia University

Based in Greater Philadelphia, Arcadia University is a top-ranked private university offering more than 65 fields of undergraduate study and graduate programs ranging from the doctoral level to certificate programs. A national leader in international education and study abroad, Arcadia offers a one-week preview for first-year and transfer students; summer, semester, and one-year study abroad programs for undergraduate students; and international field and research experiences for graduate students.

Arcadia's international programs have been consistently ranked among the top regional universities in the north by *U.S. News & World Report.* In 2015, Arcadia was ranked first in the nation by the Institute of International Education's *Open Doors* report for the percentage of undergraduate students participating in a study abroad experience, marking the sixth time in seven years the university has earned the top spot. The College of Global Studies at Arcadia University is the first college of its kind dedicated to the delivery and development of education abroad and offers more than 130 international education programs in 15 countries around the world. Approximately 70% of Arcadia students study abroad over the course of their academic careers.

The Arcadia University Knights compete on 19 varsity sports teams in the Commonwealth Conference of the Middle Atlantic Conferences. Esteemed lecturers visit campus to present their latest work, speak on advancements in their fields, and share observations on their careers. The centerpiece of campus is Grey Towers Castle, recognized on the National Register of Historic Places. Select first-year students are housed in traditional and suite-style dorms in the castle, offering them a rare living arrangement during their college experience.

Information courtesy of Arcadia University

Belmont University

As a Christian community of learning and service, Belmont University takes pride in offering educational experiences that support and promote exploration of God's purpose for each of our lives. We foster high-impact practices through our curriculum and our dedication to service learning and work that makes a difference in our community, locally and globally. Our campus is intentional in its commitment to develop students' leadership capacities and to engage them in meaningful experiences that will position them to transform the world.

Ranked fifth in the Regional Universities South category and praised for the eighth consecutive year as for its innovative practices by *U.S. News & World Report*, Belmont offers more than 80 areas of undergraduate study. Current leading majors include music business, nursing, audio engineering technology, and biology. Belmont has spent more than $500 million in the past 15 years adding new academic and residential spaces to campus or upgrading older facilities to provide students with the absolute best learning environments possible. As Nashville's university, we take our commitment to the community seriously and strive to enrich, as we are enriched, by our Nashville location.

Belmont's general education program, the BellCore, is anchored in four distinct yet integrated learning practices, starting with the First Year Seminar, building through Linked Cohort courses with an experiential learning component, a junior-level course featuring team-based learning, and the Senior Capstone. The BellCore engages students in inquiry and analysis, interdisciplinary critical thinking, and teamwork while also allowing them to follow their own design for integrated learning. Believing real experience helps students find careers, most academic programs augment curricula with internships and service-learning projects.

Study away, study abroad, service projects, and mission trips are also hallmarks of the Belmont experience. Whether as a graduate pharmacy student building a medical records database in Ecuador or as part of a team of new students painting the bleachers at a Nashville high school, Belmont students are guided by faculty and staff who place students at the center of all they do and encourage—on campus and by example—a lifetime filled with learning and service.

Information courtesy of Belmont University

California Lutheran University

Founded in 1959, California Lutheran University (Cal Lutheran) is a comprehensive liberal arts–focused institution and is home to more than 4,100 undergraduate and graduate students from more than 66 countries and represent a wide variety of faiths and backgrounds.

Cal Lutheran's dedicated, accomplished faculty work with small classes of students who are open minded about ideas, people, and faith, and seeking to grow as individuals. Through experiences inside and outside the classroom, everyone at Cal Lutheran is committed to helping students pursue their passions to discover their purpose so that they can transform their communities and the world.

Traditional undergraduates have their choice of 35 majors and 34 minors. Cal Lutheran's bachelor's degree for professionals program is designed to meet the needs of adult students. Master's and doctoral degrees, credentials, and certifications are offered through the Graduate School of Education, School of Management, Graduate School of Psychology, and Pacific Lutheran Theological Seminary.

The university's main 225-acre Thousand Oaks campus, ideally situated between Los Angeles and Santa Barbara, is complemented by four satellite centers in Oxnard, Santa Maria, Westlake Village, and Woodland Hills. Pacific Lutheran Theological Seminary's campus is located in Berkeley.

Cal Lutheran is one of 26 colleges and universities affiliated with the Evangelical Lutheran Church in America. It is accredited by the Western Association of Schools and Colleges Senior Colleges and Universities Commission. Cal Lutheran's 21 intercollegiate athletic teams compete in the Southern California Intercollegiate Athletic Conference and the National Collegiate Athletic Association Division III.

Information courtesy of California Lutheran University

Drury University

At the Civic Engagement Summit, students and their community partners described the impact of their partnerships. The prehealth students found their work with a clinic serving low-income families inspiring. "How so?" they were asked. "It taught me compassion," one student said. "I didn't realize all the obstacles that people face to get access to health care. We need to make it easier for them to get healthy and stay healthy."

Across the room, students of architecture in a service-learning studio described their work to revive a low-income neighborhood on an urban stretch of old Route 66. "What did you take away from this project?" they were asked. "We did not have any idea this part of town had such a rich history," they responded. Their community partner quickly added, "People in this neighborhood used to feel forgotten. These students made us feel like our lives matter again."

Stories such as these underscore the value of a Drury education. The experiences we offer students are designed to cultivate the virtues and values that make us fully human, and to prepare us intellectually to solve problems and to care deeply about those problems. It is an education of hearts and minds.

The Drury Core: Engaging Our World, now in its fourth year, signals our commitment to educating the whole person in several ways. All students are required to complete two engaged learning requirements, immersion learning experiences aimed at developing either global learning, community engagement, or leadership and professional abilities.

These values have earned Drury national recongnition:

- Missouri's No. 1 Midwest Regional University in *U.S. News & World Report 2014*, a list we have been at or near the top of since 1999
- A Top 100 Best Value Private University for 2015 (*Kiplinger's*)
- One of the best colleges in the Midwest (*The Princeton Review*)
- 63% of students completed an internship in 2013–14
- 97.3% of 2014–15 postgraduation survey respondents stated they were either employed, in grad school, or taking a gap year within six months
- One of 13 colleges nationwide named Institutions of Excellence in the First College Year by the Policy Center on the First Year of College

---

Information courtesy of Drury University

Hamline University

Founded in 1854, Hamline University is the first university in Minnesota. It is affiliated with and rooted in the values of the United Methodist Church; grounded in the liberal arts; and fosters intellectual curiosity, civic engagement, inclusion, and social justice in its students.

Ranked first in its class in Minnesota and designated by *U.S. News & World Report* as among "America's Best Colleges" and "Great Schools, Great Prices," Hamline University is a leader in high-impact practices for students (undergraduate research collaborations with faculty, internships, and service-learning projects), innovative teaching and learning, and personal attention from top-rated professors. Hamline alumni include distinguished scientists, business leaders, educators, judges, Rhodes Scholars, Fulbright Scholars, and Truman Scholars. The Institute for International Education recognizes Hamline for the percentage of students who study abroad. Students participate in service-learning projects internationally. Hamline is also recognized in the U.S. President's Higher Education Community Service Honor Roll in all four areas of civic engagement.

Graduate faculty bring real-world experience to master's and doctoral programs in business, education, and creative writing. The School of Business includes master's programs in business, non-profit management, and public administration. The School of Education is a leader in urban education, environmental education, and English as a second language programs. Faculty in the master of fine arts program include Newbery, Printz, and National Book Award winners and finalists. Hamline is also affiliated with the innovative Mitchell Hamline School of Law.

Hamline University prepares students who do "all the good they can" and who will be the leaders for tomorrow's world.

Information courtesy of Hamline University

John Carroll University

As a Jesuit Catholic university, John Carroll University's mission is to inspire individuals to excel in learning, leadership, and service in the region and around the world. John Carroll has focused on graduating students of intellect and character in the Jesuit tradition of educational excellence for more than 125 years. Founded as St. Ignatius College in 1886, the institution was renamed John Carroll University in 1923, in honor of the first archbishop of the Catholic Church in the United States.

Today John Carroll offers more than 70 distinct majors to approximately 3,700 students through the College of Arts and Sciences and the John M. and Mary Jo Boler School of Business. The university is consistently recognized for its academic rigor as a top 10 master's university in the Midwest according to *U.S. News & World Report*'s "Best Colleges" guide.

Service to others is a defining element of the John Carroll experience, with the majority of students embracing local, national, and global volunteerism, immersion, and study abroad opportunities.

The beautiful 64-acre campus is located in the Cleveland suburb of University Heights. The university offers state-of-the-art facilities, including the Dolan Center for Science and Technology, which houses the departments of biology, chemistry, physics, mathematics and computer science, and psychology.

Famous alumni include Don Shula (1951), the "winningest coach" in National Football League history, and the late Tim Russert (1972), former moderator of NBC's *Meet the Press*, known for his integrity and his passion for truth in political journalism.

Information courtesy of John Carroll University

Manhattan College

Located in New York City, Manhattan College is a Lasallian Catholic institution that embraces men and women of all faiths, cultures, and traditions. Manhattan College was founded in 1853 by the de La Salle Christian Brothers, a religious teaching order established by Saint John Baptist de La Salle, who provided education to disadvantaged children in seventeenth-century France.

Following de La Salle's example, the college is committed to offering an affordable, quality education to its more than 3,500 students from nearly 50 countries. Educating both the heart and the mind, faculty and staff help to foster a Lasallian experience by integrating de La Salle's five core principles into classroom learning, extracurricular activities, civic engagement, volunteering, learning and living environments, study abroad, and professional experiences.

Manhattan College provides unparalleled opportunities for its students through experiential learning in New York City. With a large alumni mentor program and a small student-to-faculty ratio of 12:1, students gain real-world skills through internships as well as through hands-on research and field trips. Manhattan College offers more than 40 major programs of undergraduate study in liberal arts, business, education and health, engineering and science, along with continuing and professional studies for nontraditional learners. Within the past five years, the Manhattan College has added new majors in all of these fields, including art history, environmental studies, environmental science, business analytics, and radiologic technology.

Manhattan College is consistently ranked in national surveys as a leading college for return on investment (ROI), value of a degree, and graduate salaries. Brookings Metropolitan Policy Program ranked Manhattan College in the top 10 nationwide for ROI. Last year, the college also ranked No. 17 in *U.S. News & World Report's* America's Best Colleges in the North category.

In 2014, Manhattan College opened the doors of its $45 million Raymond W. Kelly '63 Student Commons, which connects the college's north and south campuses and offers increased space and programming, a state-of-the-art fitness center, new dining options, and much more. With the completion of the student commons, Manhattan College is taking steps to launch its next Campus Facilities Master Plan, which will significantly enhance science, technology, engineering, and math facilities on campus.

Information courtesy of Manhattan College

Nazareth College

Nazareth is an independent comprehensive college located in Rochester, New York. Since its founding in 1924, Nazareth has prepared its graduates for meaningful lives by providing courses of study in the liberal arts and professional programs. In the past decade, the college has built on this tradition by developing a distinctive core curriculum that emphasizes the relevance of the liberal arts and sciences to life and work. The core curriculum is an integrative studies approach to learning that allows students the flexibility to tailor their courses based on their individual interests.

Nazareth offers the Bridge Plan, a program of mentored career planning throughout each student's time at Nazareth. Students integrate well-structured experiential learning opportunities with their academic course of study. Experiential learning opportunities can take the form of community service, service-learning, internships, a leadership program, study abroad, student creative activity and research, or the many field and clinical placements that are embedded in professional programs.

Our School of Management, home to the Center for Entrepreneurship, prepares students with internship opportunities and coursework developed in collaboration with an advisory council of business experts. The School of Education offers multiple certifications in early childhood and adolescence education, including an unusual program that earns candidates four certifications in four years. In our School of Health and Human Services, programs in the allied health professions engage students in hands-on, interprofessional practice in the newly renovated York Wellness and Rehabilitation Institute. The College of Arts and Sciences offers a breadth of liberal arts programs in the humanities, social sciences, visual and performing arts, foreign languages and literatures, as well as math and science, housed in the state-of-the-art Peckham Hall, home to the Integrated Center for Math and Science.

Nazareth strives to be a community of engaged scholars. Our overseas programs in more than 20 countries prepare students to be global citizens. Nazareth has been ranked among the top producers of U.S. Fulbright Scholars, with 20 Fulbrights awarded to Nazareth students in the past five years. The Center for Civic Engagement and the Hickey Center for Interfaith Studies and Dialogue serve local and global communities. Nazareth was also named one of just five presidential award winners in the 2013 President's Higher Education Community Service Honor Roll and was a finalist for the 2011, 2014, and 2015 awards.

Information courtesy of Nazareth College

North Central College

North Central College is a comprehensive college of the liberal arts and sciences committed to academic excellence; a curriculum that balances liberal arts learning with professional application; a climate that emphasizes leadership, ethics, values, and service; and a caring environment of small classes and personalized attention. Founded in 1861, North Central is proud of its United Methodist heritage and supports a diverse and inclusive campus population. The college is a founding member of NAC&U.

Enriching a thriving culture of inquiry are integrative, interdisciplinary academic opportunities and programs of distinction like the College Scholars Honors Program and annual symposium for undergraduate research. A faculty distinguished for its teaching is supported with 14 endowed chairs and five Ruge Fellowships. A world-class science center opening in 2017 will enhance the academic experience.

Unique programs and opportunities build on the college's character, mission, and location: Chicago Term and urban and suburban studies; faculty-led December Term courses on campus and worldwide; East Asian studies with Japanese and Chinese language tracks; a Middle Eastern and North African studies program with Arabic language; teacher preparation for high-need schools; study fellowships for student travel and research; and award-winning cocurricular activities such as Model United Nations, Mock Trial, and Forensics. The college's radio station, WONC-FM 89.1, has been named the best in the country. Many ministry and service programs build leadership skills and engagement through spiritual activities, team building, and volunteerism.

Study abroad opportunities, a growing international student population, an academic focus on global studies, and an active International Club resulted in North Central's receiving the prestigious Paul Simon Award for Comprehensive Internationalization.

Resident students appreciate a growing choice of residence hall options and a campus located adjacent to the vibrant community of Naperville, Illinois. Cultural, recreational, and professional opportunities abound near campus and in Chicago, just 30 minutes away via train.

With 25 athletic programs, 31 team national championships, 600 student athletes, and an undergraduate population averaging 2,700, athletics is a point of great pride. The college is an National Collegiate Athletic Association Division III leader for its balance of academics, leadership development, and athletic performance. Faculty mentors frequently attend athletic team events on campus and out of town.

Information courtesy of North Central College

Ohio Northern University

Ohio Northern University's ambitious, pioneering attitude has been alive since the very beginning. The school started with a single person and a single idea when, in the late 1860s, Henry Solomon Lehr decided to expand the town's education system by building a college.

Ohio Northern's evolution from a normal school (one that only trained teachers) to a true university was no small feat. It reflects the impressive power of Lehr's philosophy of low tuition, flexible curriculum, and equality in education. By 1885 the original focus on professional and liberal education for teachers was broadened to include programs in business, engineering, pharmacy, and law.

We believe that our students deserve an education that prepares them for the world ahead. We believe that values can't be overlooked. We believe that college should be treated as an investment. And we believe that time spent at Ohio Northern paves the way for the rest of a student's life.

Ohio Northern is a place where students have the freedom to explore all areas of education and the flexibility to find their own paths. Low student-to-teacher ratios mean our students work closely with instructors to think critically, creatively, and entrepreneurially; communicate effectively; gain practical experience; solve problems collaboratively; and act as ethical and responsible members of a global community. It's simple, really. Students who are able to explore their interests create more meaningful experiences for themselves and others.

At Ohio Northern, we constantly strive for excellence in academics, even if that means redefining it. That's why we focus on high-impact learning. Our students learn by doing—through internships, community outreach, and more. Hands-on learning, mentorships, and student-guided research projects are essential parts of every Polar Bear's journey.

Along the way, Ohio Northern students move toward their careers long before they graduate—and our alumni successes prove it. It's no coincidence that our 93% placement rate for graduates has beaten the national average for the past seven years. Whether students dream of becoming a Fulbright scholar, a U.S. senator, or an Academy Award winner, Ohio Northern will prepare them to launch their future from a strong foundation.

Information courtesy of Ohio Northern University

Pacific Lutheran University

Pacific Lutheran University (PLU) purposefully integrates the liberal arts, professional studies, and civic engagement in the beautiful Pacific Northwest. With distinctive international programs and close student-faculty research opportunities, PLU helps its 3,300 students from all faiths and backgrounds discern their life's vocation through course work, mentorship, and internships at world-class businesses and institutions in the Puget Sound area. Founded in 1890 by Norwegian pioneers, PLU continues the distinctive tradition of Lutheran higher education through its commitment to the advancement of knowledge, thoughtful inquiry and questioning, the preparation of citizens in service to the world, and to its ongoing reform. Located in the Parkland neighborhood of Tacoma, Washington, PLU is set in a region that also offers vast opportunities for outdoor recreation, culture, and sports.

To support students and faculty as they explore life's big questions and engage in fulfilling and meaningful work, the university established the Wild Hope Center for Vocation. A distinctively hopeful exploration, the search for vocation that faculty and students undertake together endures even in the face of the untamed and unpredictable nature of the world in which we live.

Information courtesy of Pacific Lutheran University

Roger Williams University

Many universities prefer to dwell in tradition, relying on history as evidence of their ability to meet the needs of students and families. Yet, in a higher education climate rife with uncertainty, Roger Williams University (RWU) stands out as an innovator for its distinctive approach.

With campuses in Bristol and Providence, Rhode Island, RWU is home to 4,000 undergraduates, more than a dozen graduate programs, a thriving School of Continuing Studies, as well as Rhode Island's only law school.

A leading independent coeducational university offering more than 45 majors in the liberal arts and the professions, RWU guarantees every undergraduate the opportunity for at least one experiential education project as part of his or her course of study to apply classroom theory to practice and ensure that every graduate has the skills employers want. Many of these projects take shape in community-engaged settings including an array of public interest initiatives, from a thriving oyster gardening program helping to revive Narragansett Bay ecologically and economically, to legal clinics and pro bono representation to Rhode Islanders in need. Students and faculty also work through the Community Partnerships Center and the Business Partnerships Center, which provide nonprofit organizations, government agencies, and small businesses with assistance in addressing real-world challenges.

Through its Affordable Excellence initiative, the university has taken a leadership position on cost and debt. A series of tuition freezes and guarantees (a locked-in tuition rate for each student, assuming an on-time graduation) since 2012 has made an RWU education more affordable and accessible for students from myriad backgrounds.

Each of these initiatives—as well as the university's long-held commitment to excellence in education, academic accomplishment, and community service through intellectual exchange, critical thinking, inclusiveness, and innovation—has served as a building block for RWU's core purpose: to strengthen society through engaged teaching and learning.

Information courtesy of Roger Williams University

Samford University

Samford University is Alabama's top-ranked private university and provides nationally recognized academic programs rooted in its historic Christian mission. Founded in 1841 and located in suburban Birmingham, Samford is the 87th oldest institution of higher learning in the United States. It enrolls 4,933 students from 44 states, the District of Columbia, and 25 countries in 10 academic units: arts, arts and sciences, business, divinity, education, health professions, law, nursing, pharmacy, and public health.

In 2014, *U.S. News & World Report* ranked Samford third among regional universities in the South and third in the South for best undergraduate teaching. Samford is the top-ranked university in Alabama according to Forbes's 2014 college rankings. Samford also has been nationally ranked for academic programs, value, and affordability by such prestigious publications and rankings as *Kiplinger's Personal Finance, The Princeton Review,* and Colleges of Distinction, among others.

Samford offers 32 undergraduate and graduate/professional degrees. There are 155 undergraduate majors, minors, and concentrations. Graduate/professional degrees are offered in business, divinity, education, environmental management, law, music, nursing, and pharmacy. A new College of Health Sciences is bringing many new undergraduate and graduate/professional programs online in the near future.

The faculty-to-student ratio is 1:12, and no classes are taught by teaching assistants. Among Samford's 46,000-plus alumni are more than 60 U.S. congressmen, seven state governors, two U.S. Supreme Court justices, four Rhodes Scholars, multiple Emmy and Grammy award–winning artists, two national championship football coaches, and recipients of the Pulitzer and Nobel Peace prizes.

The university fields 17 varsity sports—8 men's and 9 women's—that participate at the NCAA Division I level in the Southern Conference.

Information courtesy of Samford University

St. Edward's University

Six years ago, when my oldest son, Michael, began to consider colleges, he had three top requirements for his ideal school: a strong program in his field of interest, the chance to be involved in club sports, and easy access to a city (like Austin, Texas) that's creative, energetic, and fun.

To me, there were many more variables to consider: class size, programs, success rates, costs and aid, location, distance from home! My son was making a life-changing decision—one that would involve rigorous research, consideration and parental support, not to mention a good deal of serendipity.

After careful deliberation (and to my delight), Michael chose to attend St. Edward's University. There, he shined. He entered as a gregarious, sports-crazy, average student, excited about majoring in criminal justice. He emerged as a mature, thoughtful, self-assured adult, who is now in his second year of law school.

When I reflect on Michael's four years on the hilltop, I'm grateful for (and a little awed by) the community of caring people who influenced his education and growth: his professors who made a point of getting to know him as a person and who challenged him, listened to him, encouraged him, mentored him, and made him accountable for doing his best work. His internships with the district attorney's office in Austin that helped him gain job skills in his major. His friends and classmates who opened his world to new ideas, places and interests.

The examples go on, too numerous to list here. But the main insight I want to share with you is this: At St. Edward's, your student won't be just a face in the crowd. Personal experiences with a human touch are ingrained in the university's liberal arts culture and Holy Cross tradition. It's a place where learning and achievements happen in ways that support the goals and needs of each student and build confidence, resilience, and important life and career skills—the outcomes we all wish for our children.

Sincerely,
Sallie Small
Mother of Michael '14, Aaron '17, and Spencer Small
San Diego, CA

Information courtesy of St. Edward's University

The Sage Colleges

Margaret Olivia Slocum Sage founded Russell Sage College in 1916 with the mission to educate women to be scholars, professionals, and leaders. For 100 years Russell Sage has prospered, and the women's college has grown to include the coeducational undergraduate Sage College of Albany; the graduate schools of education, health sciences, and management; the School of Professional and Continuing Education; and Russell Sage Online.

Interdisciplinary academics, community service, international engagement, and artistic and athletic endeavors shape the educational experience at The Sage Colleges. Sage's academic programs focus on science, technology, engineering, and math (STEM); health sciences; business; and educational leadership and develop nimble thinkers who adapt quickly in a changing job market. Students build on their majors to include a cross-section of subjects and balance classroom lessons with community engagement through service projects, academic service-learning, and work-study positions.

The Sage Colleges emphasize liberal arts core programming that supports professional and career development on two very unique campuses nine miles apart. On its historic campus in Troy, New York, Russell Sage College is committed to providing the women's college experience with the signature Women Owning Responsibility for Learning and Doing (WORLD) program, a general education program designed to create women of influence ready to lead, succeed, and continue learning. Russell Sage College is also known for its performing arts programs and the Theatre Institute at Sage. Sage College of Albany, in the capital city of New York, offers a coeducational experience with a core curriculum in Innovation Thinking, known as i.Think. Sage College of Albany undergraduates gain hands-on educational experience through internships in the capital region and beyond, including hospitals, government, private industry, technology leaders, and many other partners. The Albany campus houses the world-class Opalka Art Gallery and is known for its visual and graphic arts program. Sage offers graduate programs on both campuses and Russell Sage Online in education, health sciences, and management.

Our motto "To Be, To Know, To Do" expresses the timeless imperatives that underscore Sage's values of self-discovery and excellence, the rigorous pursuit of knowledge, and the responsibility to engage in meaningful and constructive ways in local and global communities.

Information courtesy of The Sage Colleges

University of Evansville

The University of Evansville is a private liberal arts and sciences university set on 75 acres in Evansville, Indiana. The university is a top 10 Best Regional University in the Midwest according to *U.S. News & World Report* and in the top 10% of all master's-granting institutions for social mobility, research, and service based on a *Washington Monthly* report.

The university's Schroeder School of Business, College of Education and Health Sciences, College of Engineering and Computer Science, and William L. Ridgway College of Arts and Sciences offer more than 80 different majors and 100 areas of study.

The University of Evansville is dedicated to active learning and scholarship and is committed to the liberal arts and sciences as a basis for intellectual and personal growth. It endeavors to prepare its graduates for lives of personal and professional service and leadership. The university adopts a global view in its programs and vision to help graduates succeed in an international community. Harlaxton College is the university's campus in Grantham, England.

Through its GAP program, the university's students can gain real-world experience, work with students in other majors, and earn credits while gaining marketable skills. Multidisciplinary teams of students work side by side with leading organizations on real-world issues that matter. Guided by faculty coaches and outside experts, participants produce practical outcomes for their clients. Projects have included developing a marketing and fund-raising strategy for an archeological dig in Israel; advising a global plastics manufacturer on international expansion; and improving nutrition, health, and education delivery services in rural Guatemala.

The University of Evansville is committed to quality, affordable education and was named one of the nation's top 100 best value private colleges by *Kiplinger's Personal Finance*. The Guarantee Program ensures that 100% of full-time freshmen entering in fall 2015 receive an academic scholarship, graduate in four years (or the university covers the cost of the fifth year), engage with faculty, have access to at least one internship, and have the opportunity to study abroad.

Information courtesy of University of Evansville

University of La Verne

The University of La Verne is a private, independent nonprofit institution that provides distinct, relevant, and values-based educational opportunities for the academic and personal development of its undergraduate, graduate, and adult learner students.

The university consists of four colleges—the College of Arts and Sciences, the College of Business & Public Management, the College of Education & Organizational Leadership, and the College of Law—serving 8,700 students on 11 Southern California campuses.

The University of La Verne bases its curricular and cocurricular programs on the four core institutional values of lifelong learning, civic and community engagement, diversity and inclusivity, and ethical reasoning.

This is exemplified throughout the La Verne Experience, a program that integrates curricular and cocurricular programs, pairs disparate courses and disciplines, connects and integrates continuous civic and community engagement, and culminates with a comprehensive e-portfolio in which students reflect on their experiences. Through the La Verne Experience, students receive a personalized liberal education with diverse programs and opportunities that link scholarship, service, theory, and practice at the graduate and undergraduate levels, resulting in the fulfillment of the institution's mission.

The university's student body closely reflects Southern California's diverse population. Students from traditionally underrepresented populations make up more than 53% of the university's total enrollment (41.6% Hispanic, 6.4% African American, 5% Asian American). The U.S. Department of Education has designated the University of La Verne a Hispanic-serving institution. More than 50% of the graduate and undergraduate population are the first in their families to attend college.

Among its national recognitions, *U.S. News & World Report* ranked the university's online undergraduate programs the best in California in the publication's second annual Online Education National Rankings and 13th overall out of 210 institutions numerically ranked. White House officials named the University of La Verne among the top five institutional recipients of the 2014 President's Higher Education Community Service Honor Roll in the category of interfaith and community service. Additionally, the University of La Verne earned a Carnegie Foundation Community Engagement Classification in 2015, held by only 361 institutions across the nation.

Information courtesy of University of La Verne

University of New Haven

The University of New Haven (UNH), located in West Haven, Connecticut, is one of the country's leaders in experiential learning. UNH gives its students a singular education that combines a strong liberal arts program with hands-on professional training.

A private, coeducational institution situated on an 84-acre campus, UNH has an enrollment of more than 6,700, which includes nearly 1,800 graduate students as well as more than 5,000 undergraduate students. Almost 60% of undergraduate students live in university housing.

The university's New England campus is within a short distance of Boston and New York City, giving students great access to the amenities and learning opportunities of these metropolitan areas, and the campus is just five minutes from the Connecticut shoreline.

UNH offers more than 85 undergraduate and graduate degree programs throughout five academic colleges: College of Business, Henry C. Lee College of Criminal Justice and Forensic Sciences, Tagliatela College of Engineering, College of Arts and Sciences, and Lyme Academy College of Fine Arts.

Some of the most popular programs of study include criminal justice, forensic science, national security studies, legal studies, fire science, engineering, music, music and sound recording, computer science, marine biology, sports management, graphic design, interior design, and dental hygiene.

Throughout UNH's undergraduate programs of study, students prepare for careers via faculty-mentored research. The average undergraduate classroom size is 23 students and students regularly participate in on-the-job training and hands-on experiences through co-ops and internships. They also have the opportunity to take part in enrichment programs through a comprehensive study abroad program and service-learning.

Information courtesy of University of New Haven

University of Redlands

The University of Redlands is a private, independent undergraduate and graduate institution located in the historic heart of Southern California. Founded in 1907 and situated on one of the most beautiful campuses in the region and state, Redlands is consistently ranked among the best universities in the nation. Redlands offers more than 40 undergraduate majors as well as graduate or professional programs in business, communicative disorders, education, geographic information systems, and music. The university blends liberal arts and professional education, applied and theoretical study, traditional majors and an alternative degree program.

The Johnston Center for Integrative Studies offers one of the most challenging, rewarding, transformative, and distinctive undergraduate experiences in American higher education today. The center is based on two simple ideas: that students should be allowed and even encouraged to take control of their own education, and that education is more effective when it integrates students' living and learning environments. Rather than faculty members assigning what to study and read for a course, students negotiate contracts with a faculty/peer committee, create a course syllabus tailored specifically to the individual, and receive narrative evaluations instead of grades. The Johnston Center consider knowledge less in terms of "majors" and more in terms of an intentional series of connected ideas and practices, and Johnston students are expected to learn about and clearly articulate the educational choices they make.

Also a nationally unique program, the School of Education's doctorate in leadership for educational justice (EdD) enrolls about 20 students each year, and the program's emphasis on educational justice sets it apart. As doctoral candidates learn to apply transformative leadership practices, the idea that educators from all backgrounds should have access to quality instruction, resources, and other educational opportunities is a central tenet of the program. The School of Education is also home to the Center for Educational Justice, which sponsors institutes, symposia, workshops, and other educational efforts related to social advocacy, research and policy development, and professional training on equity, fairness, care, respect, and awareness of broader societal inequities.

Information courtesy of University of Redlands

University of Scranton

The University of Scranton is a Catholic and Jesuit university animated by the spiritual vision and the tradition of excellence characteristic of the Society of Jesus and those who share its way of proceeding. The university is a community dedicated to the freedom of inquiry and personal development fundamental to the growth in wisdom and integrity of all who share its life.

Since its founding in 1888, Scranton has become a nationally respected comprehensive university. Best 377 Colleges, Best Buys in College Education, America's Best Colleges, "A Focus on Student Success"—these are just a few of the ways that the nation's leading college rankings and guidebooks consistently refer to the University of Scranton. For 21 consecutive years, *U.S. News & World Report* has ranked Scranton among the 10 top master's universities in the North. *U.S. News* has also ranked the university among America's up-and-coming schools to watch, identifying Scranton among the nation's universities making "the most promising and innovative changes in the areas of academics, faculty, student life, campus or facilities."

For 10 consecutive years, *The Chronicle of Higher Education* has also listed Scranton among the "top producers" of Fulbright awards for American students.

Scranton is a caring, nurturing community, offering undergraduate students a core curriculum rooted in the Jesuit tradition of liberal arts. Scranton communicates to students the importance of gathering, evaluating, disseminating, and applying information using traditional and contemporary methods. Scranton provides learning experiences that reach beyond the fundamental acquisition of knowledge including understanding interactions and syntheses through discussion, critical thinking, and application. This dedication to educational process promotes a respect for knowledge and a lifelong commitment to learning, discernment, and ethical decision making.

Information courtesy of University of Scranton

Valparaiso University

At Valparaiso University (Valpo), students explore concepts and ideas alongside professors who care about their success and classmates who motivate them to be their best.

Valpo is a comprehensive, selective, private, residential university with five undergraduate colleges (Arts and Sciences, Business, Engineering, Nursing and Health Professions, and Christ College—the Honors College), a graduate school, and a law school.

The College of Engineering is recognized as one of the nation's finest engineering programs by *U.S. News & World Report* and has 4-year, ABET-accredited degree programs in civil, electrical, computer, and mechanical engineering.

Located on Valpo's Indiana campus, the James S. Markiewicz Solar Energy Research Facility is one of five research facilities in the United States with a solar furnace—the only one at an undergraduate institution.

Students develop cross-cultural communication skills through organizations like Engineering Without Borders, where engineering and nursing students often collaborate to develop sustainable solutions to improve quality of life for people around the world.

In response to a rapidly growing health care industry, the College of Nursing and Health Professionals now offers programs in health care leadership, physician assistant studies, and public health, as well as traditional and accelerated nursing degrees. Preparing graduates for one of the fastest growing fields, the public health program equips students with skills to promote and protect health around the world.

Located close to Chicago, Valpo has partnerships with local and regional businesses that offer opportunities for internships and other experiential learning. The newly developed entrepreneurship minor allows students to establish a foundation in leadership, innovation, and social responsibility, and Valpo's forthcoming Entrepreneurship Center will serve the campus community as well as regional partners.

Meteorology students gain hands-on experience in the campus Weather Center and work with an array of meteorological equipment including Doppler radar. Many participate in National Weather Service programs.

Information courtesy of Valparaiso University

Wagner College

Wagner College is an innovative liberal arts college for aspiring leaders who want to live and learn on a beautiful, traditional campus; enjoy the vast resources of New York City; and connect the liberal arts with fulfilling careers.

Wagner College was founded in 1883 in Rochester, New York, as a small, specialized high school/junior college for young men preparing for the Lutheran seminary. We moved to the New York City borough of Staten Island in 1918 and evolved into a full-spectrum, coeducational, secular liberal arts college. Exponential enrollment growth following World War II led to the addition of professional and graduate programs.

The greatest transformation in the history of Wagner College came in 1997 with the adoption of our signature undergraduate curriculum, the Wagner Plan for the Practical Liberal Arts, which features three learning communities at the beginning, middle, and end of the undergraduate career—including an immersive, multidisciplinary first-year learning community—along with civic and field learning experiences and internship placements for every student. The Wagner Plan for the Practical Liberal Arts offers students an unparalleled educational experience that focuses on learning by doing, and the close-knit campus community promotes students' personal and intellectual development.

Our verdant, parklike campus is an urban oasis situated atop a hill that overlooks New York Harbor, the Statue of Liberty, and the world-renowned Manhattan skyline. It serves as an ideal base from which to explore the professional and cultural resources of one of the truly great cities of the world.

Information courtesy of Wagner College

Westminster College

Westminster College is a private, independent, and comprehensive university in Salt Lake City, Utah. Students experience the liberal arts blended with professional programs in an atmosphere dedicated to civic engagement. With the goal of enabling its graduates to live vibrant, just, and successful lives, Westminster provides transformational learning experiences for both undergraduate and graduate students in a truly student-centered environment. Faculty focus on teaching, learning, and developing distinctive and innovative programs, while students thrive on Westminster's urban Sugar House campus that is within minutes of the Rocky Mountains.

Westminster's mission is to prepare students to lead lives of learning, accomplishment, and service, as well as to help them develop skills and attributes critical for success in a rapidly changing world. First-year students participate in learning communities and service-learning opportunities; more than 85% of students participate in internships before they graduate.

Westminster has 13 graduate programs and over 42 undergraduate majors. The college enrolls approximately 2,800 undergraduate and graduate students who come from 48 states and 41 countries. The student-to-faculty ratio is 9:1.

Some offerings of note include the aviation program, with its own flight center at Salt Lake International Airport; the honors program; the McNair Scholars program; and May Term, which is free to students who enrolled full-time the previous spring and fall. In 2014, Westminster had 23 students compete in the Winter Olympic Games in Sochi, Russia—10% of Team USA. The college currently has approximately 50 student-athletes who are members of the U.S. ski and snowboard teams who attend Westminster through a tuition grant program. Westminster also takes full advantage of what *Outside* magazine called a near-perfect location for avid outdoor adventure. The college's Outdoor Recreation Program offers adventures for students year-round. At the same time, Westminster's location also affords students access to all the opportunities to explore the increasingly dynamic urban environment of Salt Lake City.

Information courtesy of Westminster College

Widener University

Widener University is a private, innovative, metropolitan university that connects curricula to societal issues through civic engagement. Dynamic teaching, active scholarship, experiential learning, personal attention, and applied leadership are all key components of the Widener experience for our students on campuses in Chester, Harrisburg, and Exton, Pennsylvania; and Wilmington, Delaware.

Since its founding in 1821, leadership development has distinguished a Widener education. Through its 190-year history, the university has graduated great leaders—people who have served as generals, members of Congress, judges, CEOs, engineers, authors, and teachers. The university's deep commitment to programs of public service coupled with opportunities for internships, co-ops, and clinics all help to prepare students for leadership and success.

Moreover, Widener's Oskin Leadership Institute offers students structured leadership development programs that encourage students to think outside their "comfort zones." A leadership minor, certificate program, scholarships and fellowships, leadership team competitions, and more, all aim to inspire students to be strategic leaders and responsible citizens who possess the character, courage, and competencies to affect positive change throughout the world. Widener encourages its students to be globally engaged citizens and leaders. Through a variety of initiatives, Widener students not only learn an international perspective but also apply their education in service to others around the world—from physical therapy and communication studies students working together to create a video series for use by physical therapists working in Chinese orphanages, to environmental science students working with coffee farmers in Costa Rica on more sustainable approaches to coffee farming.

Collectively, a Widener education provides value in the global marketplace by providing a unique combination of leadership development and experiential learning through a curriculum focused on high-impact educational practices that involve students in addressing real issues in the communities we serve.

Information courtesy of Widener University

GRADUATE PROGRAMS OFFERED BY NEW AMERICAN COLLEGES AND UNIVERSITIES MEMBERS

Member	Graduate Programs
Arcadia University	Applied behavioral analysis
	Business administration
	Counseling
	Creative writing
	Education
	English and language arts
	Forensic science
	Humanities
	International relations
	Physical therapy
	Physician assistant
	Public health
	Written communication
Belmont University	Accounting
	Audio engineering
	Business administration
	Education
	English
	Law
	Music
	Nursing
	Occupational therapy
	Pharmacy
	Physical therapy
	Sport administration

Member	*Graduate Programs*
California Lutheran University	Business Economics Education Information technology Psychology Public policy and administration Theology
Drury University	Business administration Communication Education Studio art and theory Teaching
Hamline University	Business administration Creative writing Education Law Nonprofit management Public administration
Hampton University	Applied mathematics Atmospheric science Biology Business administration Chemistry Communicative sciences and disorders Computer science Counseling Education Information assurance Medical science Nursing Pharmacy Physical therapy Physics Psychology Sport administration

Member	*Graduate Programs*
John Carroll University	Accountancy Biology Business administration Communications management Counseling Education English Humanities Laboratory administration Mathematics Nonprofit administration Premedical postbaccalaureate Psychology
Manhattan College	Accounting (offered to Manhattan College undergraduates in a five-year MBA/accountingSS program) Advanced leadership studies Applied mathematics, data analytics Business administration Engineering Instructional design and delivery Mathematics Mental health counseling Organizational leadership School building and district leadership School counseling Teaching students with disabilities
Nazareth College	American studies Art therapy Education Educational technology Higher education student affairs administration Human resources development Human resources management Integrated marketing communications Law (3 + 3 program with Syracuse University) Management

(Continues)

Member	Graduate Programs
Nazareth College	Music therapy Physical therapy Social work Speech language pathology
North Central College	Business administration Education International business administration Leadership studies Liberal studies Web and Internet applications
Ohio Northern University	Accounting Law (juris doctor) Law (JD) Pharmacy
Pacific Lutheran University	Business Creative writing Education Marriage and family therapy Nursing
Roger Williams University	Architecture Art and architectural history Business law Criminal justice Cybersecurity Historic preservation Law Leadership Literacy education Psychology Public administration
St. Edward's University	Accounting Business administration College student development Counseling Environmental management and sustainability Leadership and change Liberal arts

Member	Graduate Programs
The Sage Colleges	Applied behavioral analysis and autism Business administration Community psychology Counseling and community psychology Education and educational leadership Forensic mental health Health services administration Nursing Nutrition Occupational therapy Organization management Physical therapy Professional school counseling
University of Evansville	Athletic training Health services administration Physical therapy Physician assistant science Public service administration
University of La Verne	Accounting Business administration Child development and child life Educational counseling and educational leadership Finance Gerontology Health administration Law Leadership and management Marriage family therapy Organizational leadership Psychology Public administration Reading Teaching
University of New Haven	Big data Business administration Cellular and molecular biology Community psychology Computer science

(Continues)

Member	Graduate Programs
University of New Haven	Criminal justice Criminal justice (PhD) Cyber systems Electrical engineering Emergency management Engineering and operations management Environmental engineering
University of New Haven	Environmental science Executive MBA Fire science Forensic science Forensic technology Health care administration Human nutrition Industrial engineering Industrial/organizational psychology Investigations Labor relations MBA/MPA dual degree MBA/MSIE dual degree Mechanical engineering National security Public administration Sport management Taxation
University of Redlands	Business administration Clinical mental health counseling Communicative disorders Curriculum and instruction Educational administration Geographic information systems Higher education Information technology Leadership for educational justice (EdD) Management Music (conducting, composition, education, performance; artist diploma) School counseling

Member	*Graduate Programs*
University of Scranton	Accountancy Business administration Chemistry Counseling Education Health administration Health informatics Human resources
University of Scranton	Nursing Occupational therapy Physical therapy Software engineering Theology
Valparaiso University	Arts and entertainment administration Business administration Chinese studies Clinical mental health counseling Comparative global inquiry Computation in the sciences Cybersecurity Digital media Education Engineering management English studies and communication Health administration Humane education Information technology International commerce and policy International economics and finance Law Liberal studies
Wagner College	Accounting Business administration Education Microbiology Nursing (including DNP) Physician assistant

(Continues)

Member	*Graduate Programs*
Westminster College	Accountancy Business administration Communication Community leadership Education Mental health counseling Nursing Public health Technology commercialization
Widener University	Business administration Clinical psychology Criminal justice Education Engineering Higher education Hospitality and tourism Human sexuality Law Liberal studies Nursing Physical therapy Public administration Social work

BIBLIOGRAPHY

Almond, G. A., & Verba, S. (1989). *The civic culture: Political attitudes and democracy in five nations.* New York, NY: Sage. (Original work published 1965)

Arum, R., & Roksa, J. (2011). *Academically adrift: Limited learning on college campuses.* Chicago, IL: University of Chicago Press.

Arum, R., & Roksa, J. (2014). *Aspiring adults adrift: Tentative transitions of college graduates.* Chicago, IL: University of Chicago Press.

Association of American Colleges and Universities. (2013). *An introduction to LEAP: Liberal education and America's promise.* Washington, DC: Author.

Astin, A. W. (1993). *What matters in college: Four critical years revisited.* San Francisco, CA: Jossey-Bass.

Ayers, E. L. (2014, June). *The future of scholarship* [speech]. New American Colleges and Universities Summer Institute, University of Redlands, Redlands, CA.

Bain, K. (2012). *What the best college students do.* Cambridge, MA: Belknap Press of Harvard University Press.

Barlament, L. (2013–2014, Winter). Exploring the cosmos: Intermediate learning community. *Wagner Magazine,* pp. 2–3. Retrieved from http://wagner.edu/wagnermagazine/exploring-the-cosmos-intermediate-learning-community/

Barlament, L. (2013–2014). Starting a career path: Internship at the Clinton Foundation, New York City. *Wagner Magazine,* pp. 3–4.

Baum, S., Ma, J., & Payea, K. (2010). *Education pays: The benefits of higher education for individuals and society.* New York, NY: College Board.

Benner, P., Sutphen, M., Leonard, V., & Day, L. (2010). *Educating nurses: A call for radical transformation.* San Francisco, CA: Jossey-Bass.

Blaich, C. (2011). *How do students change over four years of college?* Retrieved from static1.1.sqspcdn.com/static/f/333946/10418206/1296073333850/4-year-change-summary-website.pdf?token=yKH6cbkLuenqm%2Fogh5Vda%2FV1liE%3D

Boyer, E. (1994, March). Creating the new American college. *The Chronicle of Higher Education, 40*(27), A48.

Bransford, J. D., Brown, A. L., & Cocking, R. R. (1999). *How people learn: Mind, experience, and school.* Washington, DC: Committee on Developments in the Science of Learning, National Research Council.

Brown, J. S., Collins, A., & Duguid, P. (1989). Situated cognition and the culture of learning. *Educational Researcher, 18*(1), 32–42.

Chambliss, D. F., & Takacs, C. G. (2014). *How college works.* Cambridge, MA: Harvard University Press.

Clydesdale, T. (2015). *The purposeful graduate: Why colleges must talk to students about vocation.* Chicago, IL: University of Chicago Press.

Colby, A., Ehrlich, T., Beaumont, E., & Stephens, J. (2003). *Educating citizens: Preparing America's undergraduates for lives of moral and civic responsibility.* San Francisco, CA: Jossey-Bass.

Collins, A., Brown, J. S., & Newman, S. E. (1989). Cognitive apprenticeship: Teaching the crafts of reading, writing, and mathematics. In L. Reskick (Ed.), *Knowing, learning, and instruction: Essays in honor of Robert Glaser* (pp. 454–460). Hillsdale, NJ: Erlbaum.

Damon, W. (2008). *Path to purpose: How young people find their calling in life.* New York, NY: Free Press.

Delbanco, A. (2012). *College: What it was, is, and should be.* Princeton, NJ: Princeton University Press.

Gallup & Purdue University. (2014). *Great jobs great lives: The 2014 Gallup-Purdue index report.* Retrieved from www.luminafoundation.org/files/resources/galluppurdueindex-report-2014.pdf

Gardner, H., Csikszentmihalyi, M., & Damon, W. (2001). *Good work: When excellence and ethics meet.* New York, NY: Basic Books.

Keeling, P., & Hersh, R. H. (2011). *We're losing our minds: Rethinking American higher education.* New York, NY: Palgrave Macmillan.

Kuh, G. D. (2008). *High-impact educational practices: What they are, who has access to them, and why they matter.* Washington, DC: Association of American Colleges and Universities.

Kuh, G. D., Schuh, J. H., Whitt, E. J., & Associates. (1991). *Involving colleges: Successful approaches to fostering student learning and development outside the classroom.* San Francisco, CA: Jossey-Bass.

Light, R. L. (2001). *Getting the most out of college.* Cambridge, MA: Harvard University Press.

Martin, R. (2007). *The opposable mind: How successful leaders win through integrative thinking.* Boston, MA: Harvard Business School Press.

McNeill, W. H. (1995). *Keeping together in time: Dance and drill in human history.* Chicago, IL: University of Chicago Press.

Mesrobian, C. (2013). *Sex and violence.* Minneapolis, MN: Carolrhoda Books.

Murchland, B. (Ed.). (1991). *Higher education and the practice of democratic politics.* Dayton, OH: Kettering Foundation.

Pascarella, E. T., & Terenzini, P. T. (1991). *How college affects students: A third decade of research.* San Francisco, CA: Jossey-Bass.

Pascarella, E. T., Terenzini, P. T., & Wolfe, L. M. (1986). Orientation to college and freshman year persistence/withdrawal decisions. *The Journal of Higher Education, 57*(2), 155–175.

Putnam, R. C. (2000). *Bowling alone: The collapse and revival of American community.* New York, NY: Simon & Schuster.

Putnam, R. C. (2015). *Our kids: The American dream in crisis.* New York, NY: Simon & Schuster.

Roels, S. J. (2014). An education for life abundant. *Liberal Education, 100*(1), 6–13.

Saltmarsh, J., & Harley, M. (Eds.). (2011). *To serve a larger purpose: Engagement for democracy and the transformation of higher education*. Philadelphia, PA: Temple University Press.

Seligman, M. E. P. (2011). *Flourish: A visionary new understanding of happiness and well-being*. New York, NY: Free Press.

Staton, C. P., Jr. (2003). *A sturdy American hybrid: Associated New American Colleges*. Macon, GA: Mercer University Press.

Students engage legislators with hope of enacting change. (2013, May 8). *What's Up @ Widener, 7*(17), 1. Retrieved from www.widener.edu/news-events/whatsup/vol_7/Vol.7Issue17.pdf

Sullivan, W. M. (2005). *Work and integrity: The crisis and promise of professional education* (2nd ed.). San Francisco, CA: Jossey-Bass.

Tinto, V. (2012). *Leaving college: Rethinking the causes and cures of student attrition*. Chicago, IL: University of Chicago Press.

Tocqueville, A. de. (1969). *Democracy in America*. (G. Lawrence, Trans.) New York, NY: Doubleday. (Original work published 1840)

ABOUT THE AUTHOR

William M. Sullivan is a senior scholar at New American Colleges and Universities as well as visiting professor at the Center for the Study of Professions at Oslo and Akershus University College in Norway. He was formerly a senior scholar at the Center of Inquiry at Wabash College and at the Carnegie Foundation for the Advancement of Teaching, where he coordinated the Preparation for the Professions Program. He is the author or coauthor of a number of books, including *Work and Integrity: The Crisis and Promise of Professionalism in America* (Jossey-Bass, 2005), *Educating Lawyers: Preparation for the Profession of Law* (Jossey-Bass, 2007), *A New Agenda for Higher Education: Shaping a Life of the Mind for Practice* (Jossey-Bass, 2008), *Habits of the Heart: Individualism and Commitment in American Life* (University of California Press, 1985, 1996), and most recently *Liberal Learning as a Quest for Purpose* (Oxford University Press, in press).

INDEX